CALL to FAITH

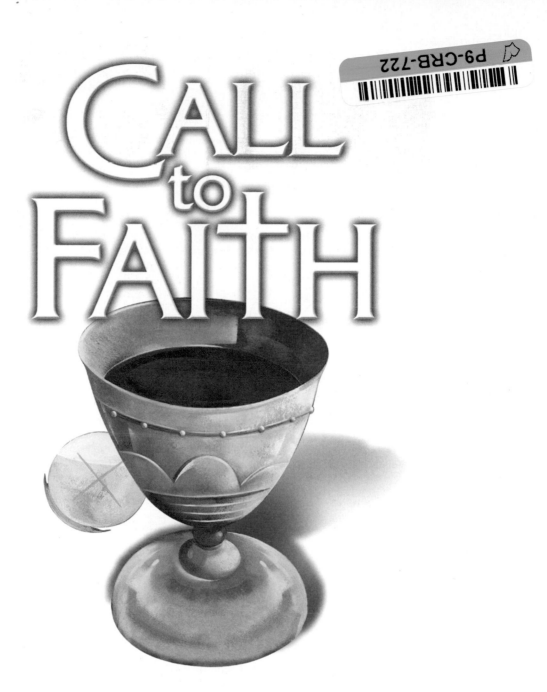

GRADE 2
Parish

OurSundayVisitor

Curriculum Division

www.osvcurriculum.com

Nihil Obstat
Rev. Richard L. Schaefer

Imprimatur
✝ Most Rev. Thomas Wenski
Bishop of Orlando
December 14, 2007

The Imprimatur is an official declaration that a book or pamphlet is free of doctrinal or moral error. No implication is contained therein that anyone who granted the Imprimatur agrees with the contents, opinions, or statements expressed.

For permission to reprint copyrighted materials, grateful acknowledgment is made to the following sources:

American Bible Society: Scriptures from the *Contemporary English Version of the Bible.* Text copyright © 1999 by American Bible Society.

Confraternity of Christian Doctrine, Washington, D.C.: Scriptures from the *New American Bible.* Text copyright © 1991, 1986, 1970 by the Confraternity of Christian Doctrine. All rights reserved. No part of the *New American Bible* may be used or reproduced in any form, without permission in writing from the copyright owner.

CRC Publications: Lyrics from "For Health and Strength" by Bert Polman. (verse 1, traditional). Lyrics © 1994 by CRC Publications.

HarperCollins Publishers: Adapted from "February 14, Saint Valentine's Day" (Retitled: "Prayer for St. Valentine's Day") in *A Book of Family Prayer* by Gabe Huck.

Hope Publishing Co., Carol Stream, IL 60188: Lyrics from "We Are the Church" by Richard Avery and Donald Marsh. Lyrics © 1972 by Hope Publishing Co. Lyrics from "Lord of the Dance" by Sydney Carter. Lyrics © 1963 by Stainer & Bell Ltd. Lyrics from "Spirit-Friend" by Tom Colvin. Lyrics © 1969 by Hope Publishing Co. Lyrics from "Jesus' Hands Were Kind Hands" by Margaret Cropper. Lyrics © 1979 by Stainer & Bell Ltd.

The English translation of the Psalm Responses from *Lectionary for Mass* © 1969, 1981, 1997, International Commission on English in the Liturgy Corporation (ICEL); the English translation of the Act of Contrition from *Rite of Penance* © 1974, ICEL; excerpts from the English translation of *Eucharistic Prayers for Masses with Children* © 1975, ICEL; the English translation of the Prayer to the Guardian Angel from *A Book of Prayers* © 1982, ICEL; excerpts from the English translation of *The Roman Missal* © 2010, ICEL. All rights reserved.

Additional acknowledgments appear on page 278.

Call to Faith Parish Grade 2 Student Edition
ISBN: 978-0-15-902275-7
Item Number: CU1371

6 7 8 9 10 11 12 015016 15 14 13 12 11
Webcrafters, Inc., Madison, WI, USA; June 2011; Job# 92519

Grade 2 Contents

Catholic Source Book

Faith in Action: Catholic Social Teaching

About You

Leader: We praise you and bless you, O God.

"Enter, let us bow down in worship;
let us kneel before the LORD
who made us."

Psalm 95:6

All: We praise you and bless you,
O God. Amen.

Activity ### Let's Begin

It's a New Year This year many exciting things will happen. You will get to know Jesus better. You will take part in parish celebrations. You will learn more about the Church.

During the year, you will spend time with your teacher and classmates. You might not know them right now. Why don't you tell them something about yourself?

What are some of your Favorite Things?

Food

Games

Color

1

About Your Faith

You will have many special times this year. Your family, friends, and the whole parish will help you follow Jesus. Together you will read Bible stories and learn about being part of the Church.

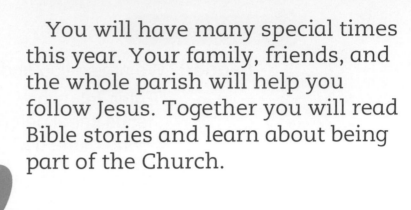

Activity Share Your Faith

Think: What is something you know about Jesus?

Share: Talk to a small group about how you learned this.

Act: Write one new thing you learned about Jesus from your group.

_____

- -

_____

_____

- -

_____

2

About Your Book

Your book has many things in it. It can help you learn more about your faith and people who live their faith. It will also show you different ways to celebrate your faith.

Activity Connect Your Faith

Seek and Find To get to know your book, look for the pictures in the signs below. Write down where you find each of them.

 Page _____

 Page _____

 Page _____

 Page _____

 Page _____

 Page _____

A Call to Faith

Gather

Pray the Sign of the Cross together.

Leader: The Lord be with you.

All: And with your spirit.

Leader: Let us pray.

Bow your heads as the leader prays.

All: Amen.

Listen to God's Word

Reader: A reading from the holy Gospel according to Matthew.

Read Mathew 4:18–22.

The Gospel of the Lord.

All: Praise to you, Lord Jesus Christ.

Reflect

How did the fishermen change that day? How does Jesus call you today?

Prayer of the Faithful

Leader: Lord, you called Simon and Andrew, and they followed you. They had faith in you and your works. With that same faith, we offer you our prayers.

Respond to each prayer with these words.

All: Lord, hear our prayer.

Signing of Foreheads

Silently pray to the Holy Spirit asking for strength to share God's word with all you meet.

Then come forward as your name is called. The leader will mark your forehead with the Sign of the Cross.

Leader: (Name), may your actions show that you have answered Jesus' call to follow him.

All:　　　Amen.

Go Forth!

Leader: Let us begin this new year with all the joy and love that comes from Christ.

All:　　　Thanks be to God.

Sing together.

We are called to act with justice,
we are called to love tenderly,
we are called to serve one another;
to walk humbly with God!

"We Are Called" © 1988, 2004, GIA Publications, Inc.

Special Days

Your family shares special days together. You may have big celebrations that include lots of people. You may celebrate birthdays and holidays with friends and people you love.

The Church shares special times together, too. These special times are called seasons. The Church's seasons celebrate events in the lives of Jesus, Mary, and saints.

Words and Actions

Hands are raised in prayer.

Heads are bowed in silence.

The Cross is honored by kneeling in front of it or kissing it.

The sign of Christ's peace is offered with a handshake.

The Sign of the Cross is marked on foreheads, hearts, and lips.

During the year, your class will use these words and actions to celebrate the different seasons.

The Church Year

Advent

Christmas

Ordinary
Time

Ordinary
Time

Lent

Easter

Triduum

Mother of Mercy

Mary is the mother of Jesus. She is the greatest of saints. The Church honors Mary with different titles. Each title tells us something about Mary. One of these titles is Mary, Our Lady of Mercy. To show mercy means to be forgiving and loving. Mary is an example of love, kindness, and forgiveness.

Acting Out of Love

Mary's actions showed love. She stayed with her cousin Elizabeth who was going to have a baby. She searched for her Son, Jesus, when he was lost in Jerusalem. Mary stayed at the cross when Jesus died. She forgave those who hurt him, as Jesus did.

Mary shows us how to love and forgive others even when we think they have made a mistake.

❓ **What is a way that you can show mercy to others?**

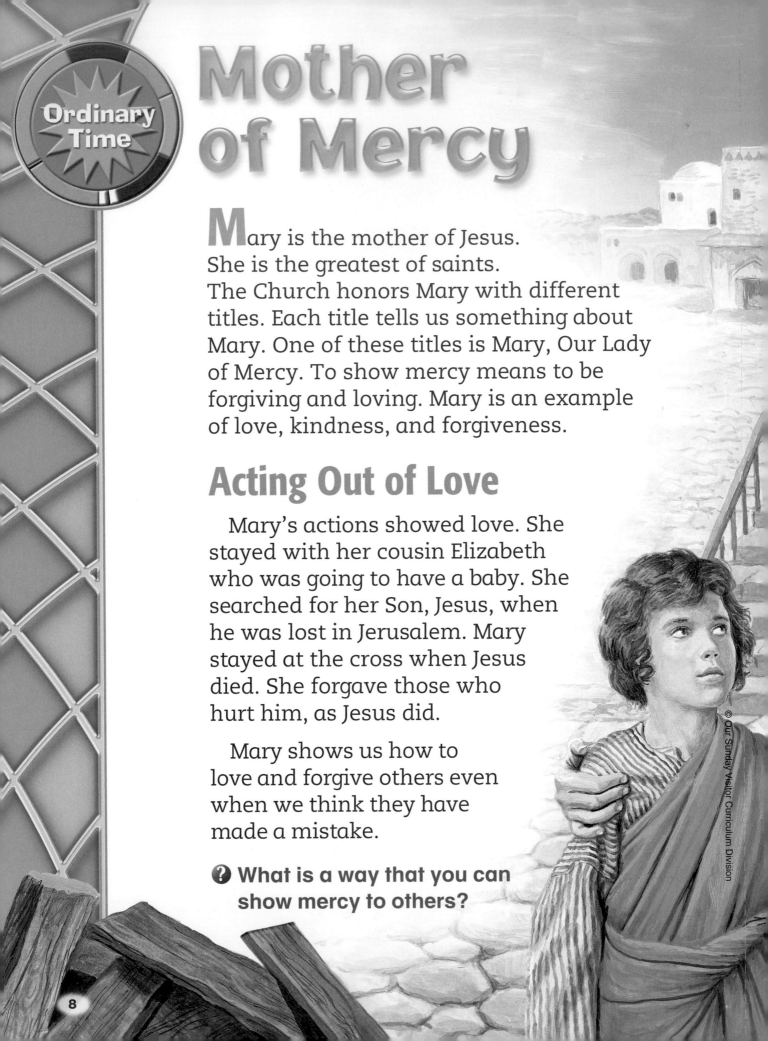

© Our Sunday Visitor Curriculum Division

Celebrate Mary

Gather

Pray the Sign of the Cross together.

Leader: Blessed be God.

All: Blessed be God forever.

Leader: Let us pray.

Bow your heads as the leader prays.

All: Amen.

Listen to God's Word

Leader: A reading from the holy Gospel according to Luke.

Read Luke 1:39–42, 45.

The Gospel of the Lord.

All: Praise to you, Lord Jesus Christ.

Reflect

What does Elizabeth say to Mary?

What is one way Mary showed her love?

 Sing together.

For your gracious blessing,
for your wondrous word,
for your loving kindness,
   we give thanks, O God.

"For Your Gracious Blessing" Traditional

Heads Bowed in Prayer

Bow your heads and think about Mary's love and kindness. Then pray together.

Leader: Hail Mary, full of grace,
the Lord is with you!
Blessed are you among
 women,
and blessed is the fruit of
 your womb, Jesus.

All: Holy Mary, Mother of God,
pray for us sinners,
now and at the hour of
 our death. Amen.

Go Forth!

Leader: Go forth to glorify the Lord by your life, as Mary did throughout her life.

All: Thanks be to God.

Sing together.

For your gracious blessing,
for your wondrous word,
for your loving kindness,
 we give thanks, O God.

"For Your Gracious Blessing" Traditional

Showing Mercy

People who show mercy notice what is happening to others. They try to see things from the other person's point of view. Merciful people think of what others need and try to help.

❓ Who do you know who needs something? How can you show mercy?

ACTIVITY

Act Out a Mercy Prayer

Work together with your class. Make gestures to go with this Mercy Prayer. Show what the words mean. Say the mercy prayer every morning.

Jesus, have mercy on me.
Mary, help me show mercy
to others today. Amen.

Waiting for Jesus

Advent is a time of waiting. The whole Church is waiting to celebrate the birth of Jesus. The Church remembers that Jesus comes to bring us hope and life.

Advent is a time to change your heart and turn toward God. It is a time to ask for God's forgiveness and mercy. Then you can celebrate Christmas with a joyful heart.

❓ What is one way you would like to change your heart as you wait to celebrate Jesus' birth?

Celebrate Advent

Gather

Sing together.

Come, O Lord, change our hearts!
Emmanuel, God is with us.

"Come, O Lord" © 1997, GIA Publications, Inc.

Pray the Sign of the Cross together.

Leader: Our help is in the name of the Lord.

All: Who made heaven and earth.

Leader: Lord, you came to gather all peoples in peace.
Lord, have mercy.

All: Lord, have mercy.

Leader: Lord, you came to show us how to be holy.
Christ, have mercy.

All: Christ, have mercy.

Leader: Lord, you will come again in glory to save your people.
Lord, have mercy.

All: Lord, have mercy.

Leader: May God have mercy on us, forgive us our sins, and bring us to everlasting life.

All: Amen.

Listen to God's Word

Leader: A reading from the holy Gospel according to Mark.

Read Mark 1:14–15.

The Gospel of the Lord.

All: Praise to you, Lord Jesus Christ.

Pray Around the Advent Wreath

Sit in silence before the Advent wreath.
Think of a way you will change your heart during Advent.

Leader: Glory to the Father, and to the Son, and to the Holy Spirit:

All: As it was in the beginning, is now, and will be forever. Amen.

Go Forth!

Leader: Let us go forth to love and serve the Lord by showing kindness to one another.

All: Thanks be to God.

Closer to God

Sometimes you may forget that God is near. You may make choices that draw you away from God. Advent is a good time to remember God's love for you. It is a time to draw closer to him.

❓ What will you do to draw closer to God during Advent?

ACTIVITY

Fill the Manger

On a separate sheet of paper, draw a manger. Underneath it write what you will do to show your love for others during Advent. Every time you show your love, draw a piece of straw in the manger. By Christmas, you will have a soft bed for the baby Jesus.

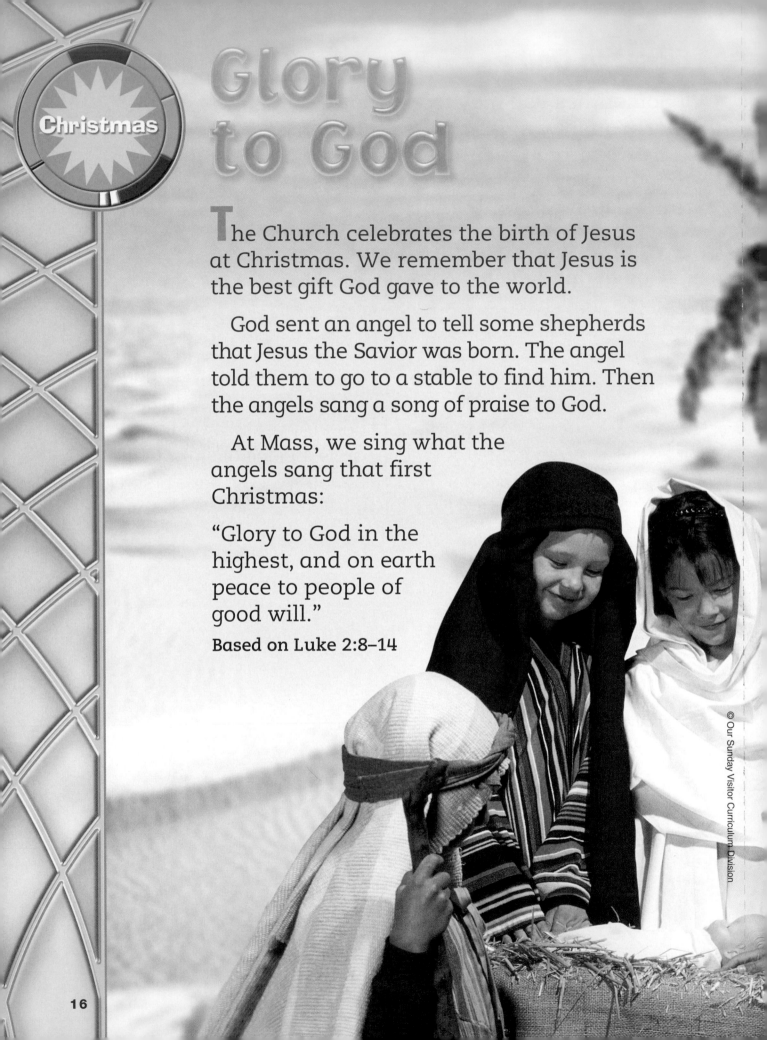

Glory to God

The Church celebrates the birth of Jesus at Christmas. We remember that Jesus is the best gift God gave to the world.

God sent an angel to tell some shepherds that Jesus the Savior was born. The angel told them to go to a stable to find him. Then the angels sang a song of praise to God.

At Mass, we sing what the angels sang that first Christmas:

"Glory to God in the highest, and on earth peace to people of good will."

Based on Luke 2:8–14

Celebrate Christmas

Gather

Sing together.

He came down that we may have love;
He came down that we may have love;
He came down that we may have love,
Hallelujah for ever more.

"He Came Down" Cameroon traditional

Pray the Sign of the Cross together.

Leader: Blessed be the name of the Lord.

All: Now and forever.

Leader: Let us pray.

Bow your heads as the leader prays.

All: Amen.

Listen to God's Word

Leader: A reading from the holy Gospel according to Luke.

Read Luke 2:8–14.

The Gospel of the Lord.

All: Praise to you, Lord Jesus Christ.

Pray Before the Crèche

Come forward and kneel before the crèche.

Leader: God, our Father, we thank you for the gift of Jesus, your Son.

All: We praise you, we bless you, we thank you.

Leader: We thank you for all the gifts of creation.

All: We praise you, we bless you, we thank you.

Leader: We ask your blessing on all your people.

All: We praise you, we bless you, we thank you.

Go Forth!

Leader: Go forth to sing of God's glory and to share his peace with others.

All: Thanks be to God.

Share the Good News

The shepherds in the fields were people of faith. They believed the good news the angel told them about Jesus.

After they saw the baby Jesus, they shared the good news with others.

❷ **What other good news about Jesus do you know? Who can you tell?**

(ACTIVITY)
Make a Good News Banner

The things you say and do can help people learn more about Jesus. As his follower, your good actions share the good news of Jesus' love. With a partner make a list of actions that show love. Then write them on a banner. Decorate your banner and hang it in the classroom.

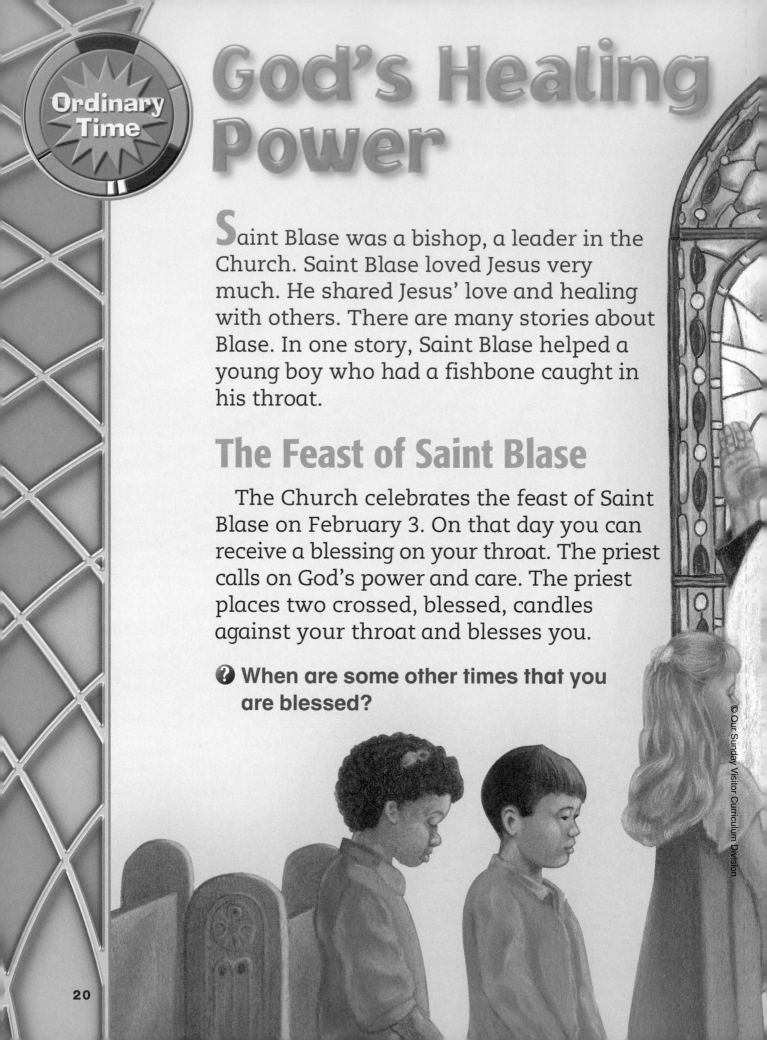

God's Healing Power

Saint Blase was a bishop, a leader in the Church. Saint Blase loved Jesus very much. He shared Jesus' love and healing with others. There are many stories about Blase. In one story, Saint Blase helped a young boy who had a fishbone caught in his throat.

The Feast of Saint Blase

The Church celebrates the feast of Saint Blase on February 3. On that day you can receive a blessing on your throat. The priest calls on God's power and care. The priest places two crossed, blessed, candles against your throat and blesses you.

❷ When are some other times that you are blessed?

Celebrate Healing

Gather

Pray the Sign of the Cross together.

Leader: Our help is in the name of the Lord.

All: Who made heaven and earth.

Leader: Let us pray.

         Bow your heads as the leader prays.

All: Amen.

Listen to God's Word

Leader: A reading from the holy Gospel according to Matthew.

         Read Matthew 8:14–17.

         The Gospel of the Lord.

All: Praise to you, Lord Jesus Christ.

Prayer of the Faithful

Leader: Let us pray for all who are sick and suffering, and for all those who care for them.

         After each prayer, answer together.

All: Lord, hear our prayer.

Leader: Let us pray in the words that Jesus taught us.

All: Our Father . . .

Blessing of Throats

Sing together.

For health and strength and
  daily food,
For neighbors, friends,
  and family,
We give you thanks, O God.
For faith and hope and
  loving care.

"For Health and Strength" © 1994, CRC Publications

As you sing, walk forward singing to receive a blessing on your throat.

Leader: Through the intercession of Saint Blase, bishop and martyr, may God deliver you from every disease of the throat and from every other illness. In the name of the Father, and of the Son, and of the Holy Spirit.

All: Amen.

Go Forth!

Leader: Let us go forth like Saint Blase, to bring God's healing Spirit to everyone we meet.

All: Thanks be to God.

Blessings

A blessing is a reminder that God loves you and that God is near. When you receive a blessing, you can thank God for his goodness to you. When you give a blessing, you remind others of God's love for them.

❓ **What are some other times that you have received a blessing?**

❓ **When do you bless others?**

⟨ACTIVITY⟩
Make a Prayer Card
Draw and color two crossed candles. Above the cross, write the names of people who are sick. Underneath the cross, write a short prayer. Ask God to bless the people who are sick and help them to be well again.

Teach Me Your Ways

The forty days of Lent are a good time to think about God's loving kindness to all people. When the people had turned from God, he sent them a Savior. No matter how many times we sin, God still invites us back into friendship with him.

Each day during Lent, the whole Church reads and listens to stories of God's love. We hear the stories of the works of Jesus. We hear about his sacrifice to save us from our sins. As we listen, we try to think of ways that we can be more loving to others.

❓ **What is a way that you want to be more like Jesus?**

Celebrate Lent

Gather

Pray the Sign of the Cross together.

Leader: O Lord open my lips.

All: That my mouth shall praise you.

Leader: Lord Jesus, you have shown us the way to the Father.

All: Lord, have mercy.

Leader: Lord Jesus, you have given us the truth.

All: Christ, have mercy.

Leader: Lord Jesus, you are the Good Shepherd, leading us to everlasting life.

All: Lord, have mercy.

Leader: May almighty God have mercy on us, forgive us our sins, and bring us to everlasting life.

All: Amen.

Listen to God's Word

Leader: A reading from the holy Gospel according to John.

Read John 3:16-17.

The Gospel of the Lord.

All: Praise to you, Lord Jesus Christ.

Signing of the Senses

Sing together the refrain.

Teach me your ways, O Lord.

"Psalm 25: Teach Me Your Ways" ©1969, 1981, and 1997, ICEL

Leader: Let us pray.
Father of our Lord, Jesus Christ, you chose us as your holy people.

All: Sing the refrain as you trace a cross on your forehead.

Leader: Jesus shared good news with others.

All: Sing as you trace a cross on your lips.

Leader: Jesus, you showed your love by forgiving and healing others.

All: Sing as you trace a cross on your heart.

Go Forth!

Leader: Father, your Son Jesus teaches us your ways. Help us to know, love, and serve you, now and forever. In Jesus' name we pray.

All: Amen.

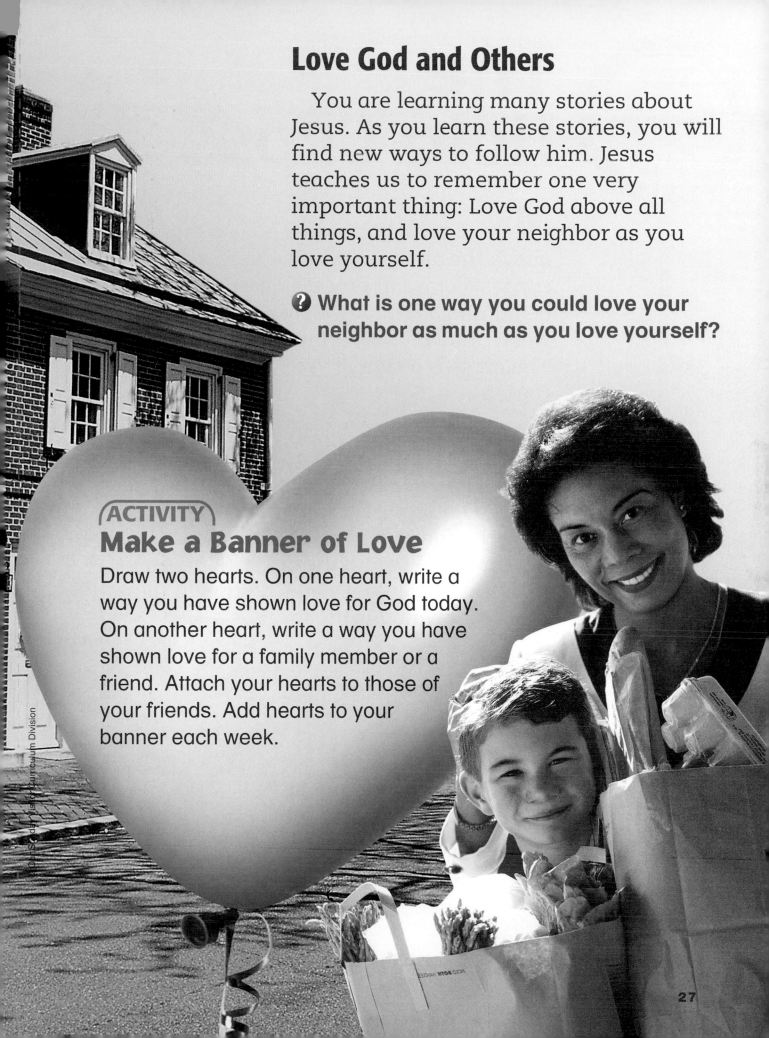

Love God and Others

You are learning many stories about Jesus. As you learn these stories, you will find new ways to follow him. Jesus teaches us to remember one very important thing: Love God above all things, and love your neighbor as you love yourself.

❓ **What is one way you could love your neighbor as much as you love yourself?**

(ACTIVITY)

Make a Banner of Love

Draw two hearts. On one heart, write a way you have shown love for God today. On another heart, write a way you have shown love for a family member or a friend. Attach your hearts to those of your friends. Add hearts to your banner each week.

The Holy Cross

Most Catholic Churches have a cross above the altar. An altar server usually carries a cross in procession at the beginning of Sunday Mass. Many people wear small crosses around their necks. The cross is a sign of your faith in Jesus Christ.

On Good Friday, the Church remembers the day that Jesus died on a cross. He died to save all people from sin and everlasting death. On Good Friday, people walk up in a procession to honor the holy cross. They bow or kneel before the cross. Sometimes they touch or kiss it. They do this to thank Jesus for giving his life for us.

❓ What is a way that you can honor the holy cross?

Celebrate the Three Days

Gather

Pray the Sign of the Cross together.

Leader: O Lord, open my lips.

All: That my mouth shall speak your praise.

Leader: Let us pray.

Bow your heads as the leader prays.

All: Amen.

Listen to God's Word

Leader: A reading from the holy Gospel according to Luke.

Read Luke 23:44-49.

The Gospel of the Lord.

All: Praise to you, Lord Jesus Christ.

Prayer of the Faithful

Leader: Let us pray for the holy People of God.

All: Lord, guide your Church.

Leader: Let us pray for our bishop, for all bishops, priests, and deacons, and for all who work in ministry in our Church.

All: Holy Spirit, guide our leaders.

Leader: Let us pray for all in our parish who are preparing for Baptism.

All: Lord, make them members of your family.

Procession to the Cross

Fold your hands and pray silently to Jesus.

Walk up slowly and in silence to honor the cross.

Bow deeply and touch the foot of the cross.

Sing together.

O how good is Christ the Lord!
On the cross he died for me.
In three days he rose again.
Glory be to Jesus! Glory be to Jesus!
Glory be to Jesus!
In three days he rose again.
Glory be to Jesus!

"O How Good is Christ the Lord" Puerto Rican traditional

Go Forth!

Leader: We believe that by his dying Christ destroyed death forever. May he give us everlasting life.

All: Amen.

Leader: May almighty God bless us, the Father, the Son, and the Holy Spirit.

All: Amen.

Helping Others

Jesus carried his cross to the place where he would die. He loved all people so much he was willing to die for them. When we do something that is difficult in order to help others, sometimes we say that we are "carrying a cross," too. We are willing to think of their needs.

❓ **What is something you have done for others, even when it was hard?**

ACTIVITY
Make a Cross

Use poster board to make a small cross to fit in your pocket. Decorate it to look like wood. Touch the cross in your pocket every time you are asked to do something that is difficult. Ask Jesus to help you, and he will!

31

A Joyful Season

Easter is always in the spring in the northern half of the world. The Easter Season lasts for fifty days. It is the most joyful season in the Church year. The Church is celebrating the Resurrection of the Lord. We sing Alleluia and ring bells.

After God the Father raised Jesus to new life, Jesus met with his followers several times. They were so happy to see him again! Then Jesus returned to his Father in heaven. But he promised to send the Holy Spirit to be with them always.

❷ Why is spring a good time to celebrate Easter?

Celebrate Easter

Gather

Pray the Sign of the Cross together.

Leader: Light and peace in Jesus Christ our Lord, alleluia.

All: Thanks be to God, alleluia.

Leader: Let us pray.

Raise your hands as the leader prays.

All: Amen.

Listen to God's Word

Sing together.

¡Aleluya, aleluya! ¡Aleluya, aleluya!
 ¡Aleluya, aleluya!
¡El Señor resucitó!
¡Aleluya! ¡Aleluya! ¡Aleluya! ¡Aleluya!
 ¡Aleluya! ¡Aleluya! ¡Aleluya! ¡Aleluya!

"Honduran Alleluia" Honduran traditional

Leader: A reading from the holy Gospel according to Luke.

Read Luke 24:13-35.

The Gospel of the Lord.

All: Praise to you, Lord Jesus Christ. Alleluia, alleluia.

The Lord's Prayer and Sign of Peace

Leader: Let us pray in the words that Jesus taught us.

Raise your hands as you pray.

All: Our Father . . .

Leader: May the God of light and peace fill our hearts and lives.

All: Amen.

Leader: Let us offer to each other a sign of the peace of Christ.

Offer one another a sign of peace.

Go Forth!

Leader: Go in peace, alleluia.

All: Thanks be to God, alleluia.

Good News

The two travelers on the road recognized Jesus when he broke the bread. How surprised they must have been. Jesus was truly alive again! The travelers could not wait to tell others.

❓ What good news can you tell others about Jesus?

ACTIVITY
Make a Card

Make an Easter greeting card to send to a relative. Decorate the front of your card. On the inside, write some good news about Jesus.

The Power of the Holy Spirit

The Holy Spirit came to the followers of Jesus fifty days after Easter. They were gathered in a room together. They missed Jesus. Jesus had gone to be with his Father in heaven. They were not sure what to do.

Then the Holy Spirit came in wind and fire. Jesus' followers were filled with joy and hope. They went out of the room and began to tell the good news of Jesus.

Everyone understood their words and many were baptized that day.

❓ **What gifts did the Holy Spirit bring to the followers of Jesus?**

Gather

Pray the Sign of the Cross together.

Leader: Light and peace in Jesus Christ our Lord, Alleluia.

All: Thanks be to God, Alleluia.

Leader: Let us pray.

Raise your hands as the leader prays.

All: Amen.

Listen to God's Word

Leader: A reading from the Letter of Paul to the Romans.

Read Romans 8:26–27.

The word of the Lord.

All: Thanks be to God.

Sing together.

God sends us his Spirit to befriend
and help us.
Recreate and guide us, Spirit-Friend
Spirit who enlivens, sanctifies,
enlightens,
Sets us free, is now our Spirit-Friend.
Spirit of our Maker, Spirit-Friend.

"Spirit-Friend" © 1987, Hope Publishing Company

Go Forth!

Final Blessing

Bow your heads as the leader prays.

Leader: May the Lord bless us and keep us.

All: Amen.

Leader: May the Lord's face shine upon us.

All: Amen.

Leader: May the Lord look upon us with kindness, and give us peace.

All: Thanks be to God, Alleluia, Alleluia.

Helper and Friend

God sent the Holy Spirit to be with us always. The Holy Spirit strengthens us when we are weak. He helps us understand Jesus' teachings. He guides us to live as followers of Christ.

❓ What can you tell others about the Holy Spirit?

ACTIVITY
A Helping Hand

A dove is a symbol of the Holy Spirit. On a separate sheet of paper write down some of the ways the Holy Spirit helps you.

Unit 1
Revelation

In this unit you will...

learn that God gave us many gifts. God's gifts tell us about what he is like. We can learn about God's gifts and his love from the Bible. Adam and Eve turned away from God. God kept loving them anyway. Jesus, God's only Son, is his greatest gift. Jesus is our Savior. He brings us back in friendship with God, his Father.

Chapter 1

Chapter 2

Chapter 3

? What do you think you will learn in this unit about God's gifts?

Chapter 1 God's Creation

Let Us Pray

Leader: We praise you with joy, O God. "Shout joyfully to God, all you on earth." *Psalm 66:1*

All: We praise you with joy, O God. Amen.

Activity Let's Begin

We Thank Thee

For flowers that bloom about our feet;

For tender grass so fresh and sweet;

For song of bird and hum of bee;

For all things fair we hear and see.

Father in heaven, we thank thee!

Ralph Waldo Emerson

• What do you want to thank God for today?

Thanks and Praise

◎ Focus What are God's gifts of creation?

David was a shepherd a very long time ago. He became a king of God's people. He wrote poems of praise and thanks to God. Many of David's poems are part of the Bible. They are called psalms. Sometimes you hear the psalms at Mass.

David often watched the sheep in the fields at night. He was amazed by the wonders of the night sky. As he looked at **creation**, he praised God for his gifts.

David was grateful, most of all, that people had been made in God's own image. This means people can think and love and make choices. Nothing else God made can do these things.

❓ What makes people different from the rest of God's creatures?

In God's Image

Humans are the most special part of God's creation. God wants you to take care of the many gifts of creation. Here is one of David's psalms about humans.

Words of Faith

Creation is everything made by God.

 SCRIPTURE Psalm 8:2, 7–9

Praise for the Creator

O LORD, our Lord,
    how awesome is your name through
        all the earth!

You have given them rule over the
    works of your hands,
        put all things at their feet:

All sheep and oxen,
    even the beasts of the field,

The birds of the air, the fish of the sea,
    and whatever swims the paths of the seas.

Psalm 8:2, 7–9

❓ **How are people responsible for animals?**

Activity — Share Your Faith

Think: What are some ways you take care of creation?

Share: Talk with a partner about these things.

Act: Plan one way to take care of God's creation this week.

Jesus and You

 **Focus** Why is Jesus God's greatest gift?

Faith Fact

The name Jesus means "God saves."

David knew that God is the Creator of everything that is good. But David was born too soon to know about God's greatest gift. God's greatest gift is his Son, Jesus.

Jesus was human, just like you, except in one way. Jesus never disobeyed God the Father. Jesus did not **sin**.

Jesus learned about God and learned how to pray from his family. He listened to Mary, his mother, and Joseph, his foster father. Jesus did what they asked him to do.

❓ **What are some other things that Jesus might have done that you also do?**

Alike But Different

While he was on earth, Jesus saw interesting things every day, just as you do. He enjoyed the flowers, the birds of the air, and the fruit trees. He learned to do new things, just as you do.

Jesus is human. He is more. He is the **Son of God** who became man. That is why you look to Jesus to learn more about God.

Activity Connect Your Faith

Find the Hidden Word Color the X's red. Color the O's blue, green, or yellow to find a name for Jesus.

Blessing Prayer

 **Let Us Pray**

Gather and begin with the Sign of the Cross.

Leader: God gave us wonderful gifts.
Let us give thanks to the Lord.

All: It is right and just.

Leader: Come, all children.
Bless the Lord.
Stand in his holy place.

All: We lift our hands.
Give praise to God.

Leader: May the Lord our God,
who made heaven and
earth, bless the world
and all that is in it.

All: Amen.

Sing together the refrain.

Lord of all, to you we raise
This our hymn of grateful praise.

"For the Beauty of the Earth" Traditional

CHAPTER 1

Review and Apply

Work with Words Fill in the blank with the correct word from the Word Bank.

1. All that God has made is called
_____
_ _ _ _ _ _ _ _ _ _ _ _ _ _ _ _
_____.

2. The greatest of all God's gifts to the
_____
_ _ _ _ _ _ _ _ _ _ _ _ _ _ _ _
world is _____.
_____
_ _ _ _ _ _ _ _ _ _ _ _ _ _ _ _

3. You can _____ for creation.
_____
_ _ _ _ _ _ _ _ _ _ _ _ _ _ _ _

4. Jesus did not _____.
_____
_ _ _ _ _ _ _ _ _ _ _ _ _ _ _ _

5. David wrote _____ of praise and thanks to God.

Activity Live Your Faith

Care for Creation Write the name of one person or thing in God's creation. Write what you can do to care for the person or thing.

_____
_ _ _ _ _ _ _ _ _ _ _ _ _ _ _ _
_____
_ _ _ _ _ _ _ _ _ _ _ _ _ _ _ _
_____

Family Faith

Catholics Believe

- God is the creator of all that is good.

- Jesus is God's greatest gift. Jesus is the Son of God.

✝ SCRIPTURE

Read Genesis 1—2:4 to learn of God's glory as the creator of everything.

GO online www.osvcurriculum.com
For weekly scripture readings and seasonal resources

Activity

Live Your Faith

Make a Creation Centerpiece Use natural objects like leaves, flowers, stones, and feathers. Add a candle to your centerpiece and put it on your dinner table. As you pray before meals, add prayers of thanksgiving for God's good creation.

People of Faith

Blessed Virgin Mary Mary was a special gift from God. God chose Mary to be the mother of Jesus, his Son. Mary was a woman of great faith. Mary is also the mother of the Church. The Catholic Church remembers Mary in every Mass. There are many prayers and feast days to give honor to Mary. The Hail Mary is the most well known prayer about the Mother of God.

▲ Mary, first century

🙌 Family Prayer

Mary, mother of God, pray for our family that we may have faith as you do. Amen.

In Unit 1 your child is learning about REVELATION.

CCC *See Catechism of the Catholic Church 319, 356, 454 for further reading on chapter content.*

Chapter 2 God's Promise

Let Us Pray

Leader: Thank You, God, for taking care of us. "You led your people like a flock."

Psalm 77:21

All: Thank You, God, for taking care of us. Amen.

Activity Let's Begin

A Trip to the Zoo One day the children from Good Shepherd Parish took a field trip to the zoo. Mrs. Walker told the children to stay together.

When the children moved on to the lion house, Bobby stayed to make faces at the monkeys.

Soon he found himself alone.

• Make up an ending for this story. Who will help Bobby find his way back to his group?

© Our Sunday Curriculum Division

Obeying God

Focus What choice did the first humans make?

Bobby chose to stay behind. God gives all people the ability to choose. The first book of the Bible tells a story about a choice made by the first humans. They are called Adam and Eve.

✝ SCRIPTURE Genesis 2:15–17; 3:1–6, 23

In the Garden

God put Adam and Eve in a garden called Eden. There they had all that they needed to live and be happy.

God told Adam and Eve that they were free to eat from all the trees in the garden, except one. God said, "When you eat from that tree, you will surely die."

A serpent also lived in the garden. The serpent said to the woman, "This is not true. God knows that if you eat that fruit, you will know what is good and what is bad."

Eve saw the tree's fruit and ate some. She gave some to Adam. He ate it, too.

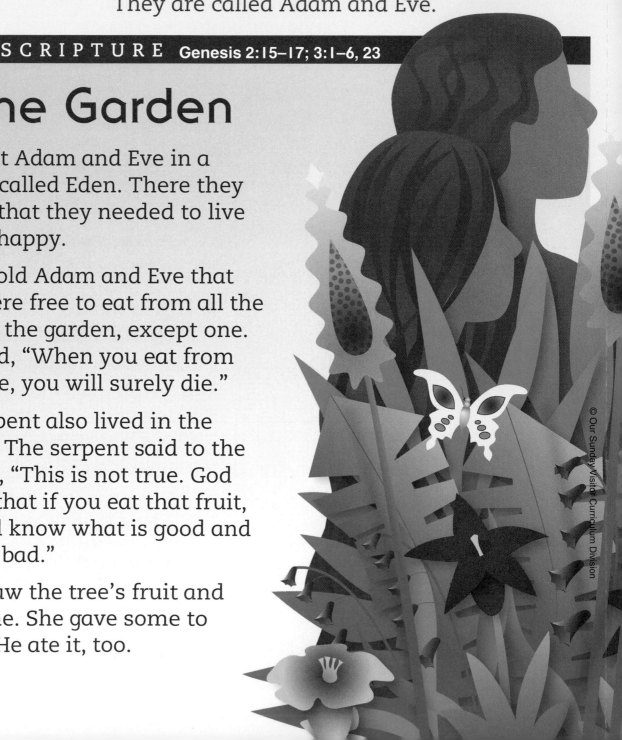

The first humans chose to do what they knew God did not want them to do. So God sent them away from the Garden of Eden.

Based on Genesis 2:15–17; 3:1–6, 23

Adam and Eve's choice to disobey God is called **original sin**.

❓ **What did the first humans lose when they chose to disobey God?**

Words
of Faith

Original sin is the first sin committed by the first people.

Activity — Share Your Faith

Think: What do you think God wants children your age to do?

Share: Talk about ways you can obey God at school.

Act: Draw yourself choosing to obey God. Label your picture.

God's Promise

 **Focus** What are some names for Jesus?

God did not turn away from Adam and Eve. Instead, God promised to send a **savior**. God promised that the savior would lead all people back to friendship with him.

God kept his promise. He sent his own Son to be the Savior of all people. Jesus came into the world to save all people and lead them to God. Jesus wanted people to love God and to be happy with God again.

❓ What are some ways you can show God you love him?

Jesus, the Savior

Jesus wanted the people to understand he is the Savior. Jesus told a story to show that he is like a shepherd and his followers are like sheep. Shepherds care for their sheep and lead them to grass and water. Shepherds make sure their sheep do not get lost.

❓ Why are shepherds important?

The Good Shepherd

Jesus said, "I am the good shepherd. A good shepherd lays down his life for the sheep. A hired man ... sees a wolf coming and leaves the sheep and runs away, and the wolf catches and scatters them. ... He ... has no concern for the sheep. I am the good shepherd, and I know mine and mine know me."

From John 10:11–14

❓ **How is Jesus like a shepherd?**

Words of Faith

The **Savior** is the one sent into the world to save people who were lost through sin and to lead people back to God.

Activity Connect Your Faith

✏️ **Write Names for Jesus** Choose one other name that you know for Jesus. Write a sentence that tells why Jesus is called by that name.

_____

- -

_____

- -

_____

Prayer of Praise

 Let Us Pray

Gather and begin with the Sign of the Cross.

Sing together the refrain.

My shepherd is the Lord,
nothing indeed shall I want.

"Psalm 23: My Shepherd is the Lord" © 1969, 1981, and 1997, ICEL

Leader: The Lord is my shepherd,
nothing shall I want.

All: Sing the refrain.

Leader: You lead me to green pastures.
You lead me to clear waters.
You guide me on the right path.

All: Sing the refrain.

Leader: I am not afraid.
Your rod and staff give me courage.

All: Sing the refrain.

Leader: Your goodness and kindness
follow me all the days of my life.

All: Sing the refrain.

Based on Psalm 23

Work with Words Write the letter of the correct words from the Word Bank to complete each sentence.

WORD BANK
a. savior
b. original sin
c. Shepherd
d. Jesus
e. friendship

1. The choice of the first humans to disobey God is called _____.

2. God promised to send a _____.

3. The savior God sent was _____.

4. Jesus is the Good _____.

5. Jesus brings people back into _____ with God.

Activity — Live Your Faith

✏️ **Circle Good Actions** Which actions lead to God? Write a good action that you will do.

_____

I will _____

_____

_____.

Pray

Be kind

Tell a lie

Family Faith

Catholics Believe

- God sent his Son, Jesus, to bring all people back into his friendship.

- Jesus is the Savior and the Good Shepherd.

SCRIPTURE

Read Psalm 23:1–4 for a description of the ways God guides us.

GO online www.osvcurriculum.com
For weekly scripture readings and seasonal resources

Activity

Live Your Faith

Keep on the Path Talk about the way God shepherds your family. Ask each person to name something God does for him or her. Then name something that someone in the family does to help keep family members on the right path.

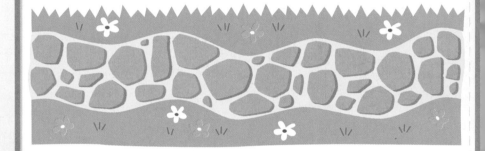

People of Faith

▲ Saint Juan Diego, 1474–1548

Juan Diego lived in Mexico. On a December day, Juan was walking to church. He met a beautiful woman who looked Mexican and spoke Juan's language. She said that she was the Mother of God and that her son was Jesus, the Savior. This woman is called Our Lady of Guadalupe. Today she is honored as the mother who protects people. Saint Juan's feast day is December 9. The feast of Our Lady of Guadalupe is December 12.

Family Prayer

Saint Juan, ask God to help us take care of others as a good shepherd does. Amen.

In Unit 1 your child is learning about REVELATION.

Chapter 3 God's Word

Let Us Pray

Leader: Thank you, God, for taking care of us.
"Your word is a lamp for my feet,
a light for my path." Psalm 119:105

All: Thank you, God, for taking care of us. Amen.

Activity Let's Begin

Share Stories Keisha brought Grandma Gibbs to the computer room at the library.

Keisha said, "Sit right here, Grandma. Our family Web site is ready to go. Just click here to get started."

Grandma did, and soon the family tree popped up on the screen.

"We can find out all about our family," Keisha said. "We can share our stories, too."

• What is a family story you like to share?

God's Stories

 **Focus** **What is the Bible?**

God wants people to believe in him and to love him. He wants you to remember his special love. Here is a story about God's love for his people.

A Sign of Love

Once God told Noah to build a large boat called an ark. He told Noah and his family to put all different kinds of animals on the ark, too. A great flood came, and the rains poured down for forty days. Noah's family and the animals were safe on the ark.

Then the rains stopped and the sun came out. Noah praised God for saving his family. God promised that he would always take care of his people. The rainbow was a sign of God's promise.

Based on Genesis 6–9

❓ **What are some other signs of God's love?**

The Bible

You can find stories of God's love in a special book called the Bible. The **Bible** is the word of God written in human words. God guided the human writers to write about him and his saving actions. In the Bible God tells you about himself and his plan for you. Another name for the Bible is Scripture.

The Bible has two parts. The **Old Testament** is the first part of the Bible. It is about the friendship between God and his people before the birth of Jesus. In this part of the Bible there are history books, law books, poetry, stories, and songs. The story of Noah's Ark is in the Old Testament.

© Our Sunday Visitor Curriculum Division

Words of Faith

The **Bible** is the word of God written in human words.

The **Old Testament** is about God and his people before Jesus was born.

Activity

Share Your Faith

Think: What is one thing you know about God? Write it here.

_____

- - - - - - - - - - - - - - - - - - -

_____

Share: Talk with a partner about how you learned this.

Act: This week ask family members to tell you something they know about God.

59

Jesus' Message

Focus When can you read or hear stories from the Bible?

Jesus knew the stories of God and his people. Jesus told many stories also. These stories helped people know and love God the Father. Jesus helped people love God by his actions, too.

✝ **SCRIPTURE** Matthew 4:23–25

Jesus Teaches

Jesus went all around Galilee. He taught in the synagogues where the Jewish people studied Scripture and prayed. He told people about the good news of God's kingdom. He healed many people who were ill.

Jesus became well known all across the land. People from different cities came to hear Jesus teach. They brought their friends who could not walk, and Jesus cured them. Large crowds followed Jesus wherever he went.

Based on Matthew 4:23–25

❓ **Why do you think great crowds followed Jesus?**

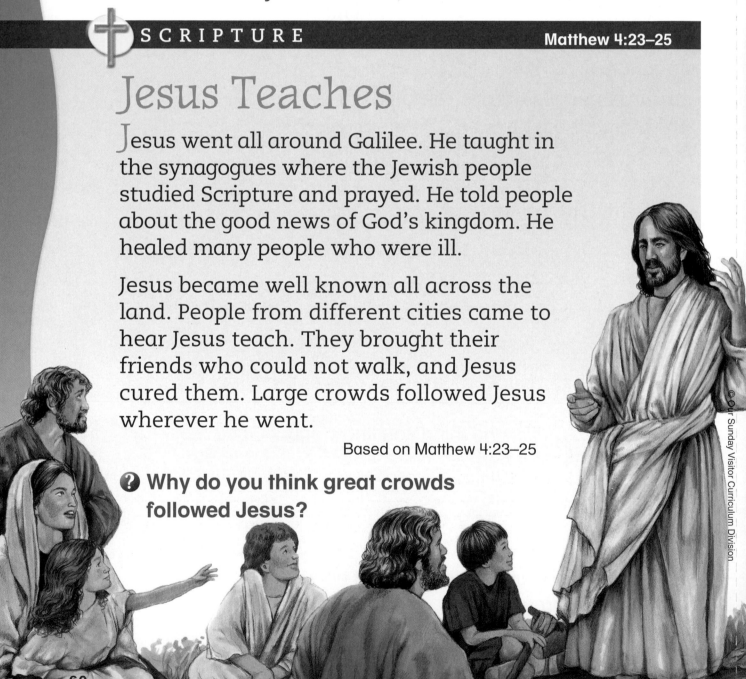

Read About Jesus

You can learn about Jesus by reading the New Testament. The **New Testament** is the second part of the Bible. It is about the life and teaching of Jesus and his followers. The first four books are called Gospels. There are also letters written by Jesus' followers to the new Christians.

Words of Faith

The **New Testament** is about the life and teachings of Jesus and the early church.

Listen to God's Word

Every Sunday during Mass, you hear readings from the Old and New Testaments. You also hear God's word when you read Bible stories with your family. You read or act out some of these stories during your religion class. Often you hear Bible stories or psalms when you pray with your class.

❓ **Where have you heard stories about Jesus?**

Activity — Connect Your Faith

Write About Jesus Imagine you are talking to a group of younger children. What would you say to them about Jesus? Write three words that tell about him.

_____

_____

_____

_____

_____

Pray with God's Word

 **Let Us Pray**

Gather and begin with the Sign of the Cross.

Leader: The Lord be with you.

All: And with your spirit.

Leader: Let us pray.
Bow your heads as we pray.

All: Amen!

Reader: A reading from the holy Gospel according to Saint Mark.

Read Mark 6:53–56.
The Gospel of the Lord.

All: Praise to you,
Lord Jesus Christ!

Sing together.

Guiding me, guarding me,
the Lord is by my side;
guiding me, guarding me,
the Lord upholds my life.

"Psalm 121" © 1969, 1981, and 1997, ICEL.

Review and Apply

A **Work with Words** Circle the correct answer.

1. The Bible has _____ parts.

    three　　　　　**two**　　　　　**four**

2. There are _____ Gospels in the Bible.

    two　　　　　**four**　　　　　**seventy-three**

3. The Old Testament is about _____.

    God's plan　　　**the Church**　　　**Jesus**

4. The New Testament has four books called _____.

    letters　　　　　**Gospels**　　　　　**stories**

B **Check Understanding** Write your answers on the lines.
When do you hear stories from the Bible?

_____

_____

_____

_____

_____

Activity　Live Your Faith

Draw A Picture Think about a time when you listened to God's word. Draw a picture of where you were and label it.

Catholics Believe

- God tells his people about himself through the Bible.

- The Bible is God's word written by humans.

✝ SCRIPTURE

Matthew 13:1–9,18–23 is about listening to God's word. Read the story together and talk about what it teaches.

GO online **www.osvcurriculum.com**
For weekly scripture readings and seasonal resources

Activity

Live Your Faith

Make a Collage As a family, talk about the ways you have each followed Jesus and acted kindly.

- From magazines, cut out pictures or photos of people acting in loving ways.

- Use the pictures and photos to make a collage.

- Write a title for your family collage.

GLUE

People of Faith

▲ Saint Luke, first century

Luke traveled a long way to tell others about Jesus. He sailed over the seas and walked trails. Luke and his followers had many stories about Jesus. These stories became the Gospel according to Luke. This Gospel tells how Jesus cared about people who were poor, sick, and lonely. It includes many of Jesus' stories about God's mercy and the kingdom of God. Saint Luke's feast day is October 18.

Family Prayer

Saint Luke, pray for us that we may share God's word with others, especially people who are poor, sick, and lonely. Amen.

In Unit 1 your child is learning about REVELATION.

Unit 1 Review

A **Work with Words** Complete each sentence with the correct word from the Word Bank.

1. The Old and New Testaments make up

   _____

   the _____.

2. You are made in the image and likeness

   _____

   of _____.

3. God promised to send a _____.

4. God's greatest gift is _____.

5. _____ is all that God made.

B **Check Understanding** Circle the correct answer.

6. Who told the story of the Good Shepherd?

   David   John   Jesus

7. What is God's word written by humans?

   a book   the Bible   God

8. Who wrote the psalms?

   David   Mary   Jesus

9. Which part of the Bible is about Jesus?

   New Testament   Psalms   Old Testament

10. Who guided the Bible writers?

    humans   Adam   God

Unit 2
Trinity

In this unit you will...

learn about each Person of the Holy Trinity. God the Father loves and cares for us as a faithful parent. We can trust and rely on God the Father. Jesus, the Son of God, sets an example for us with his life and teachings. God the Holy Spirit guides the Church and helps us to be holy.

Chapter 4

Chapter 5

Chapter 6

What do you think you will learn in this unit about God?

Chapter 4
God the Father

 **Let Us Pray**

Leader: Loving Father, remember us always.

"As a father has compassion on his children,
so the LORD has compassion on the faithful."

Psalm 103:13

All: Loving Father, remember us always. Amen.

Activity Let's Begin

Parents

Parents
Kind, patient,
Teaching, guiding, loving.
They're always there for me.
Friends.

• Who loves you? Tell about that person.

Care for God's Children

◉ Focus How does God care for you?

This is a story about a priest. He made a home for children who had no parents to love and care for them.

A BIOGRAPHY

St. John Bosco

Lorenzo and Giovanni huddled alone in the shadows. They heard mothers and fathers calling for their children. Nobody called Lorenzo or Giovanni.

Father John Bosco found the boys cold and in the dark. He brought them home. They told Father John that many other children lived alone on the streets.

"I will start a home for the children of the streets. I will teach them how to read, fix things, and pray," said Father John.

Father John helped many children who were homeless to feel loved. He taught them that God is everyone's Father. After he died, he was named a **saint**.

❓ What do you think Father John's home for children was like?

God the Father

Father John Bosco treated the young children like they were his own. He showed them love and taught them about God, like Jesus did.

Jesus taught about his Father's great love. God cares for everything and everyone. God loves you as a good parent does.

✝ **SCRIPTURE**

I will never forget you.
  See, upon the palms of my hands
    I have written your name.

Isaiah 49:15–16

❓ **How do you know that God cares for you?**

Residents of Don Bosco Orphanage in Los Palos, East Timor.

Activity Live Your Faith

Think: What are some ways God cares for you?

Share: With a partner, talk about ways you can thank God.

Act: Trace the outline of your hand. Write a thank-you prayer to God.

The Father's Love

 **Focus** **What does it mean to trust in God?**

Jesus told people not to worry too much. He said that God the Father wants you to have everything you need.

 **SCRIPTURE** Matthew 6:25–32

Count on God

Do not worry about what you will eat or wear. Life is more important than food and clothing. Look at the birds in the sky. They do not plant their food, they do not gather grain, yet your heavenly Father feeds them. Are you not more important than they? Learn from the way the wild flowers grow. They do not work or spin, but they are beautiful. If God so cares for grass of the field, how much more will he take care of you? Do not worry. Your heavenly Father knows what you need.

Based on Matthew 6:25–32

❓ **What help do you need?**

Trust in God

Jesus always called God "Father." You call God "Father" because he created you and cares for you. Jesus told his followers to pray to the Father for whatever they might need. In your **prayer**, you will be speaking to God the Father as Jesus did.

Jesus knew that you can always **trust** God. You can be sure that God loves you and wants what is best for you. God, your loving Father, is always listening.

Words of Faith

Prayer is talking to and listening to God.

To **trust** is to believe in and depend on someone.

Activity — Connect Your Faith

✏️ **Write An Asking Prayer** Write down some of the things that you and others need.

God our Father,

_____

_____

_____

_____

_____

Amen.

Asking Prayer

 **Let Us Pray**

Gather and begin with the Sign of the Cross.

Leader: Let us pray for those who need God's help.

All: Lord, hear our prayer.

Leader: For people who have lost their homes,
let us pray to the Lord.

All: Lord, hear our prayer.

Leader: For people who are far from their families,
let us pray to the Lord.

All: Lord, hear our prayer.

Leader: For help to care for others as Jesus did,
let us pray to the Lord.

All: Lord, hear our prayer.

Sing together.

Jesus' hands were kind hands,
doing good to all,
healing pain and sickness,
blessing children small.
washing tired feet,
  and saving those who fall;
Jesus' hands were kind hands,
doing good to all.

"Jesus' Hands Were Kind Hands"
© 1979 Stainer & Bell Ltd.

A **Work with Words** Fill in the blank with the correct word from the Word Bank.

1. God _____ for everyone.

2. Jesus taught you to call God the _____.

3. God loves you like a good _____.

4. You can always _____ God.

5. _____ is talking to and listening to God.

B **Make Connections** Write one way that God takes care of people.

_____

_____

_____

Activity Live Your Faith

Make a Calendar Think about needs that you or others have. Make a one-week calendar. Write one need for each day. Each day, think of a need, then ask God for help.

Family Faith

Catholics Believe

- You can call God "Father" because he created you and cares for you like a good parent.

- You can trust in God because he loves you.

SCRIPTURE

In Matthew 6:19–21 you can read what Jesus teaches about real treasure.

GO online **www.osvcurriculum.com**
For weekly scripture readings and seasonal resources

Activity

Live Your Faith

Start a Prayer Chain Make strips of colored paper. Each day, choose something to give to God's loving care. Write it on a colored strip, and attach it to the chain. The chain will remind you that your prayers are with God. So don't worry!

▲ Blessed Julian of Norwich, 1342–1420

People of Faith

Julian prayed to God as a Father and a dear Friend. She called God Mother and Brother, too. Julian said that the whole world was like a small hazelnut held in God's hand. Everything would be just fine because God cares for everything and everyone. Julian spent her life in prayer, fasting, study, and counseling others. Her feast day is May 13.

Family Prayer

Blessed Julian, carry our prayer to God. He calls us by name. He holds us in the palm of his hand. Amen.

In Unit 2 your child is learning about the TRINITY.

CCC See Catechism of the Catholic Church 322, 2780–2782 for further reading on chapter content.

Let Us Pray

Leader: Father, help us to know your Son.
"You are my son;
today I am your father."

Psalm 2:7

All: Father, help us to know your Son. Amen.

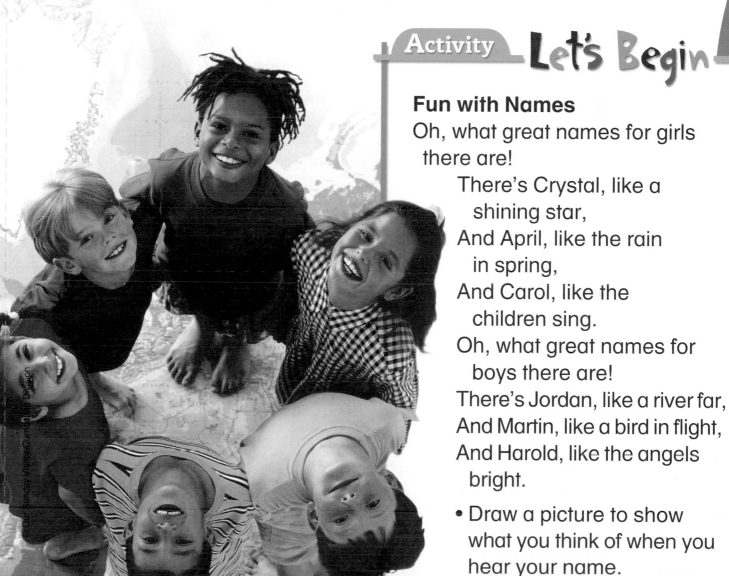

Activity Let's Begin

Fun with Names
Oh, what great names for girls there are!

There's Crystal, like a
shining star,
And April, like the rain
in spring,
And Carol, like the
children sing.
Oh, what great names for
boys there are!
There's Jordan, like a river far,
And Martin, like a bird in flight,
And Harold, like the angels
bright.

• Draw a picture to show
what you think of when you
hear your name.

© Our Sunday Visitor Curriculum Division

A Special Name

 **Focus** Who is the Savior of the world?

All names have special meanings. Long ago, God sent his only Son to earth. God sent him to show all people how they should live. God chose Mary to be his Son's mother. His Son had a special name.

✝ SCRIPTURE Luke 1:26–38; 2:1–11

Son of God

God sent his angel, Gabriel, to Mary in the town of Nazareth. The angel said, "Behold, you will give birth to a son. You shall name him Jesus. He will be great and will be called Son of the Most High."

Mary didn't understand how this could happen to her. The angel said in reply, "The holy Spirit and the power of the Most High will come over you. Therefore the child to be born will be called holy, the Son of God."

Mary told the angel, "May it be done to me as you say."

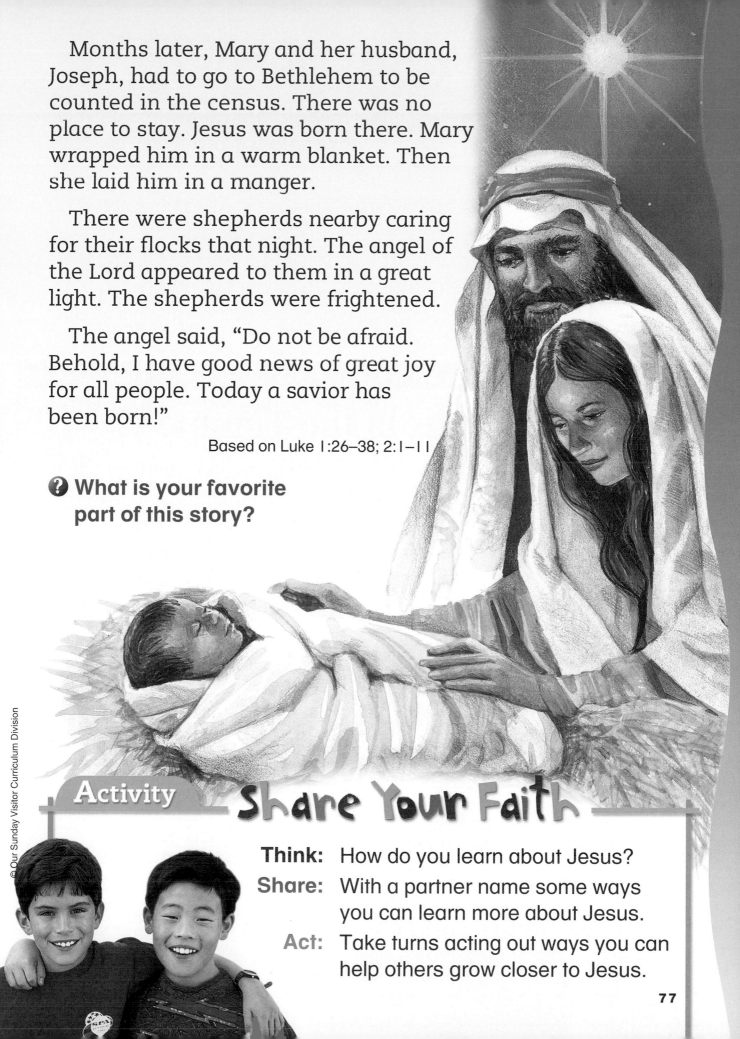

Months later, Mary and her husband, Joseph, had to go to Bethlehem to be counted in the census. There was no place to stay. Jesus was born there. Mary wrapped him in a warm blanket. Then she laid him in a manger.

There were shepherds nearby caring for their flocks that night. The angel of the Lord appeared to them in a great light. The shepherds were frightened.

The angel said, "Do not be afraid. Behold, I have good news of great joy for all people. Today a savior has been born!"

Based on Luke 1:26–38; 2:1–11

❓ What is your favorite part of this story?

Activity Share Your Faith

Think: How do you learn about Jesus?

Share: With a partner name some ways you can learn more about Jesus.

Act: Take turns acting out ways you can help others grow closer to Jesus.

© Our Sunday Visitor Curriculum Division

77

Who Is Jesus?

 **Focus** How did Jesus set an example for others?

Mary and Joseph brought Jesus back to Nazareth where he grew up. Together they are called the **Holy Family**. Jesus learned and played. He was very much like all children. Jesus was also very different from all other humans. He was the Son of God.

✝ SCRIPTURE
Luke 2:41–52

Jesus in the Temple

Once when Jesus was twelve, Mary and Joseph took him to Jerusalem for a holy day. On their way home Joseph and Mary noticed that Jesus was not in the crowd. They were very worried. They went back to Jerusalem to find him.

They found Jesus sitting with wise teachers in the **Temple**. Jesus' questions and answers amazed everyone.

Jesus came back to Nazareth and obeyed his parents. He grew in age, in learning, and in holiness.

Based on Luke 2:41–52

❓ **What is one thing Jesus might have told the wise teachers about God?**

Jesus Begins His Work

When Jesus was thirty years old, he went to see his cousin John. John wanted all sinners to turn toward God. He baptized them with water in the Jordan River.

SCRIPTURE
Matthew 3:13–17

Baptism of Jesus

One day, Jesus asked John to baptize him. Jesus never sinned. But he wanted to set an example for others. After Jesus' baptism, the Holy Spirit came down on him in the form of a dove. Then a voice from heaven said, "You are my beloved Son. I am pleased with you."

After this, Jesus taught about God his Father and shared his Father's love with everyone.

Based on Matthew 3:13–17

❓ How can you share God's love with people?

Activity — Connect Your Faith

✏️ **A Good Example** Jesus set a good example. Write one way you can set a good example for others.

_____

_____

_____

_____

Words of Faith

The **Holy Family** is the name for Jesus, Mary, and Joseph.

The **Temple** was the holy building in Jerusalem where the people came to worship God.

Prayer of Praise

 **Let Us Pray**

Gather and begin with the Sign of the Cross.

Leader: Today let us praise God and give him thanks for his greatest gift, Jesus.

Sing together the refrain.

Sing, sing, praise and sing!
Honor God for everything.
Sing to God and let it ring.
Sing and praise and sing!

"Sing, Sing, Praise and Sing!" © 2000,
GIA Publications, Inc.

Sing the refrain after each reader.

Reader 1: For Mary, who said "yes."

Reader 2: For Joseph, who cared for Jesus.

Reader 3: For telling us that Jesus is your beloved Son.

Leader: Let us pray.

Bow your heads as the leader prays.

All: Amen.

Check Understanding Complete each sentence in Column 1 with the letter of the correct words from Column 2.

Column 1	Column 2
1. Jesus is the _____.	**a.** the Holy Family
2. _____ told Mary about being the Mother of God's Son.	**b.** John
3. _____ is the savior of the world.	**c.** Son of God
4. _____ was Jesus' cousin.	**d.** Jesus
5. Mary, Joseph, and Jesus are _____.	**e.** the angel Gabriel

Activity   Live Your Faith

Draw a Way to Obey How can you obey parents or teachers?

Family Faith

Catholics Believe

- Jesus is the beloved Son of God.

- Jesus is the Savior of the world.

SCRIPTURE

Read Luke 9:18–20 to find out who Peter thought Jesus was.

GO online **www.osvcurriculum.com**
For weekly scripture readings and seasonal resources

Activity

Live Your Faith

Follow Jesus' Example Jesus obeyed Mary and Joseph, and he worked humbly as he grew. He is an example of holiness in daily life. As a family make a list of ways to respect one another. Post it on the refrigerator. At the end of the week, talk about ways you did or did not respect and love one another.

People of Faith

▲ **Saint Peter, first century**

Peter, or Simon, was a fisherman when Jesus called him to be an Apostle. Jesus chose Peter to be the leader of his other followers. Jesus named him Peter, or "the rock" on which Christ would build his Church. Peter traveled all the way to Rome to tell people about Jesus. He died for his faith in Jesus. Saint Peter's feast day is June 29.

 ## Family Prayer

Saint Peter, pray for us that we may follow Jesus as you did. Amen.

Chapter 6 God the Holy Spirit

Let Us Pray

Leader: Holy Spirit, be with us always.
"May your kind spirit guide me."
Psalm 143:10

All: Holy Spirit, be with us always. Amen.

Activity Let's Begin

Windy Day

When wind whistles and blows, feathers ruffle, leaves rustle, butterflies flutter by, water ripples, sails billow.

- What else happens when the wind whistles and blows?

Father, Son, and Holy Spirit

Focus What is the Holy Trinity?

Faith Fact

In the language of the Jewish people, the word for Spirit means wind.

You cannot see the wind, but you know that it is there. You cannot see the Holy Spirit either, but you can see what the Spirit does.

✝ SCRIPTURE

John 14:15–26

The Promise

Jesus knew he would be returning to his Father in heaven. He wanted his followers to continue his work.

Jesus promised his followers, "The Father will send the Holy Spirit. The Holy Spirit will be with you always. The Spirit will teach you everything you need to know. The Spirit will remind you of everything I have told you."

Based on John 14:15–26

❓ What did Jesus promise his followers?

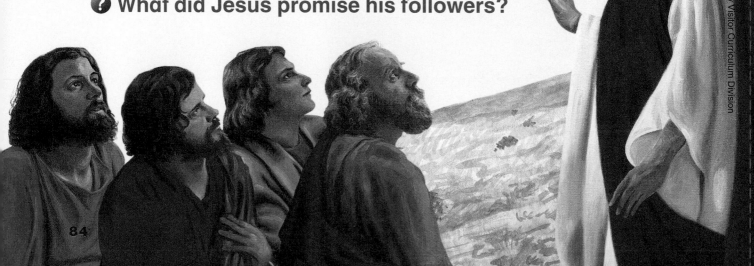

84

Three in One

Jesus teaches you that God is the Father of all. Jesus is the Son of God. And the Holy Spirit, sent from the Father and the Son, is also God.

But there are not three gods. There is only one God, who is Father, Son, and Holy Spirit. The Church's name for the three Persons in one God is the **Holy Trinity**.

- God the Father is the first Person of the Holy Trinity.

- Jesus, the Son of God who became man, is the second Person of the Holy Trinity.

- God the Holy Spirit is the third Person of the Holy Trinity.

Believing in the Holy Trinity is the most important part of your faith. You show your belief in the Holy Trinity every time you make the Sign of the Cross.

© Our Sunday Visitor Curriculum Division

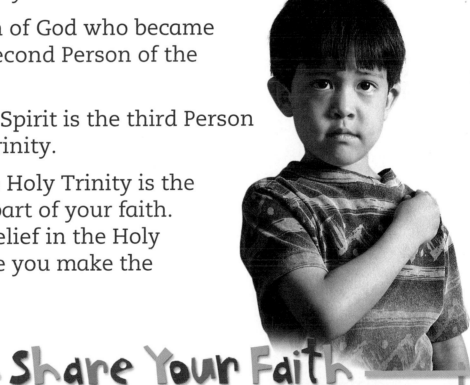

Words of Faith

The **Holy Trinity** is the three Persons in one God—Father, Son, and Holy Spirit.

Activity — Share Your Faith

Think: How do you think this picture shows the Trinity?

Share: Talk about this in small groups.

Act: Design a banner that has your own symbol for the Holy Trinity.

The Holy Spirit With Us

 **Focus** How does the Holy Spirit guide the Church?

Before Jesus returned to heaven, he told his followers his plan for them.

✝ SCRIPTURE Acts 1: 4–5, 8; 2:2

The Spirit Comes

While meeting his **disciples**, Jesus told them not to leave Jerusalem. He wanted them to wait for the promise of the Father that he had told them about. He said, "You will receive power when the holy Spirit comes upon you, and you will be my witnesses in Jerusalem . . . and to the ends of the earth."

The disciples stayed in Jerusalem and prayed. Soon the Holy Spirit came.

Suddenly a noise like a strong driving wind came from the sky, and it filled the entire house in which they were meeting.

Based on Acts 1:4–5, 8; 2:2

❓ How did the disciples know that the Holy Spirit had come?

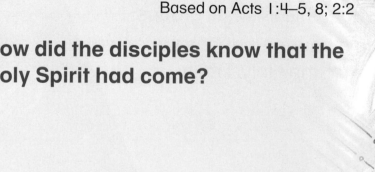

The Spirit Today

The Holy Spirit does not come into the Church today like a strong wind. Jesus does keep his promise to send the Holy Spirit to you, too. The Holy Spirit comes today through the Church's sacraments and prayer.

The Holy Spirit guides the Church and makes Jesus' disciples holy. The Holy Spirit helps you make good decisions. The Holy Spirit helps you become a more loving person.

Disciples of Jesus

Jesus' disciples are in every part of the world. The Holy Spirit teaches them how to pray. As with the first disciples, the Spirit helps today's disciples remember and understand the stories of Jesus. You are learning to be a disciple of Jesus.

Words of Faith

Disciples are people who choose to follow Jesus.

Activity Connect Your Faith

Be a Disciple At each place on the map, write one good action the Holy Spirit can help you do.

Prayer for the Holy Spirit

 Let Us Pray

Gather and begin with the Sign of the Cross.

 **Sing together the refrain.**

Come Lord Jesus, send us your Spirit,
   renew the face of the earth.

Come Lord Jesus, send us your Spirit,
   renew the face of the earth.

"Send Us Your Spirit" © 1981, 1982, 1987, GIA Publications, Inc.

Leader: Let us sing as we ask Jesus to send the Holy Spirit to us each day.

In our family . . .

All: Sing the refrain.

Leader: With our classmates . . .

All: Sing the refrain.

Leader: In all that we say and do . . .

All: Sing the refrain.

Leader: We ask this in Jesus' name.

All: Amen.

Review and Apply

Work with Words Fill in the blank with the correct word or words from the Word Bank.

WORD BANK
wind
pray
Holy Trinity
decisions
promise

1. What showed Jesus' disciples that the Holy Spirit was in the room with them?

   _____

   _ _ _ _ _ _ _ _ _ _ _ _ _ _ _ _ _ _ _

   _____

2. The three Persons in one God is the

   _____

   _ _ _ _ _ _ _ _ _ _ _ _ _ _ _ _ _ _ _

   _____ .

   _____

   _ _ _ _ _ _ _ _ _ _ _ _ _ _ _ _ _ _ _

3. The Holy Spirit helps you _____.

   _____

   _ _ _ _ _ _ _ _ _ _ _ _ _ _ _ _ _ _ _

4. Jesus _____ to send the Holy Spirit.

5. The Holy Spirit helps the followers of Jesus make

   _____

   _ _ _ _ _ _ _ _ _ _ _ _ _ _ _ _ _

   good _____ .

Activity — Live Your Faith

Follow Jesus Put a check mark next to the actions that you will do this week.

_____ Cheer up someone who is sad.

_____ Do your homework without complaining.

_____ Pray every day.

Family Faith

Catholics Believe

- The Holy Trinity is the three Persons in one God.

- The Holy Spirit guides the Church and helps you to be a disciple.

SCRIPTURE

Acts 2:37–41 tells what happened after the coming of the Holy Spirit. Read it together.

 GO online www.osvcurriculum.com
For weekly scripture readings and seasonal resources

Activity

Live Your Faith

Holy Spirit Prayer Work together to honor the presence of the Holy Spirit in your family life. Say this prayer often.

"Come, Holy Spirit, fill the hearts of your faithful and enkindle in them the fire of your love."

People of Faith

James Healy was born near Macon, Georgia. He was the oldest of ten children. His mother was a slave, and his father was from Ireland. James and two of his brothers became the first African American Catholic priests. James listened to the Holy Spirit; he was known as one of the best preachers in New England. For twenty-five years, James was the bishop of Portland, Maine.

▲ **Bishop James Augustine Healy, 1830–1900**

Family Prayer

Heavenly Father, help us see each person as your child. Give us your love to share with all your people. Amen.

© Our Sunday Visitor Curriculum Division

Unit 2 Review

A **Work with Words** Complete each sentence with the correct letter of the words from the Word Bank.

1. People who follow Jesus are called _____.

2. Jesus promised to send the _____.

3. Listening and talking to God is called _____.

4. Jesus taught us to call God _____.

5. The three persons in one God is called the _____.

B **Check Understanding** Complete each sentence in Column 1 with the letter of the correct words or words from Column 2.

Column I	Column 2
6. The third person of the Holy Trinity is the _____.	a. Mary
7. The Mother of God's Son is _____.	b. John Bosco
8. The first Person of the Holy Trinity is the _____.	c. Holy Spirit
9. A saint who helped homeless boys is _____.	d. Jesus
10. The second Person of the Holy Trinity is _____.	e. Father

© Our Sunday Visitor Curriculum Division

Unit 3
Jesus Christ

In this unit you will...

learn that God teaches us to love as he loved. God gave his people the Ten Commandments. Jesus gave us a new commandment of love. We show love by doing good. Our conscience is a gift God gives that helps us know right from wrong. Jesus teaches us that God our Father always offers forgiveness and shows us mercy.

Chapter **7**

Chapter **8**

Chapter **9**

What do you think you will learn in this unit about forgiveness and reconciliation?

Chapter 7 Love God and Others

Let Us Pray

Leader: God, we want to follow your laws.

"With all my heart I seek you;
do not let me stray from
your commands."

Psalm 119:10

All: God, we want to follow your laws. Amen.

Activity Let's Begin

A Good Place Recess is fun. It is like a tiny vacation in the middle of the day. You get to go to the playground with your friends. You have time to run or play games or just hang around.

When everyone follows the rules, recess turns out just right. Rules help make the playground a good place.

• Name two playground rules that help make recess a good time for everyone.

God's Laws

 **Focus** What new law did Jesus give to the people?

God gave his chosen people some laws to help them. These laws are called the **Ten Commandments**. God wants you to follow these laws, too. They help you make good choices about your friendship with God and others.

THE TEN COMMANDMENTS

1. I am the LORD your God: You shall not have strange Gods before me.

2. You shall not take the name of the LORD your God in vain.

3. Remember to keep holy the LORD's day.

4. Honor your father and your mother.

5. You shall not kill.

6. You shall not commit adultery.

7. You shall not steal.

8. You shall not bear false witness against your neighbor.

9. You shall not covet your neighbor's wife.

10. You shall not covet your neighbor's goods.

THEIR MEANING

Keep God first in your life.

Always use God's name in a reverent way.

Attend Mass and rest on Sunday.

Obey your parents and guardians.

Care for yourself and others.

Be respectful of every person.

Respect other people and their property.

Respect others by always telling the truth.

Don't be jealous of other people's friendships.

Don't be jealous of what other people have.

Jesus' Commandment

Jesus learned and followed the Ten Commandments. When he grew up, Jesus taught a commandment called the Great Commandment. It includes all the other commandments.

✝ SCRIPTURE

"You shall love the Lord, your God, with all your heart, with all your being, with all your strength, and with all your mind, and your neighbor as yourself."

Luke 10:27

Jesus also gave his followers the law of love: "Love one another as I love you."

John 15:12

❓ **How can you show love?**

Words of Faith

The **Ten Commandments** are God's laws about loving God and others.

 **Activity** Share Your Faith

Think: Pick one commandment. What are some ways you follow it?

Share: Talk about it in a small group.

✏ **Act:** Write one way you can follow the commandment.

_____

_____

_____

_____

The Way of Love

◎ Focus Who is the neighbor that Jesus says we should love?

Jesus told many stories, or parables, to teach his followers that loving God means loving our neighbor.

✝ **SCRIPTURE** Luke 10:29–37

The Good Samaritan

Once a man asked Jesus, "Who is my neighbor?" Jesus told this story to answer him.

A man was going along a road alone. Robbers came and beat him up. They took everything he had and ran away, leaving him half dead.

A Jewish priest was going down the same road. When he saw the man, he crossed over to the other side of the road.

Later, someone who took care of the Temple came along. When he saw the man, he also went by on the other side.

Then a man from Samaria came along and saw the man lying on the roadside. He hurried over to help. The Samaritan bandaged the man's sores and took him to an inn. The Samaritan gave the innkeeper two silver coins to help take care of the man.

Then Jesus asked, "Which of the three was a neighbor to the robbers' victim?" The man said, "The one who treated him with mercy."

Jesus said, "Go and do likewise."

Based on Luke 10:29–37

❓ **What better choice could the Temple worker have made?**

The Good Neighbor

This story shows that a neighbor is any person who is in need. The Samaritan saw a man who needed help. He showed him kindness and respect.

Activity Connect Your Faith

Act It Out Plan a Good Samaritan skit. Make notes for each part and some props. Take turns acting out different roles.

Pray with God's Word

 **Let Us Pray**

Gather and begin with the Sign of the Cross.

Leader: The Lord be with you.

All: And with your spirit.

Reader: A reading from the Letter of Paul to the Galatians.

> **Read Galatians 5:14.**

> The word of the Lord.

All: Thanks be to God.

Sing together.

Rejoice in the Lord always,
  again I say, rejoice!

Rejoice in the Lord always,
  again I say, rejoice!

Rejoice! Rejoice! Again I say, rejoice!
  Rejoice! Rejoice! Again I say, rejoice!

"Rejoice in the Lord Always" Traditional

Check Understanding Read the list on the left. Write the letter of the actions on the right that tell about each commandment.

Commandments	Actions
_____ You shall not kill.	**a.** Say God's name with care.
_____ You shall not take the name of the LORD your God in vain.	**b.** Obey your parents.
_____ Honor your father and your mother.	**c.** Go to church on Sunday.
_____ You shall not steal.	**d.** Do no harm to yourself or others.
_____ Remember to keep holy the LORD's day.	**e.** Do not take what belongs to another.

Activity — Live Your Faith

Show Kindness What could you tell others about being kind and showing love? Finish the sentences.

1. Remember to _____.

2. Always _____.

3. Remind others to _____.

Family Faith

Catholics Believe

- The Ten Commandments are God's laws to his people.

- Jesus teaches you to love God above all things and love others as you love yourself.

SCRIPTURE

Read John 15:11–15 to find out what Jesus calls his followers.

GO online **www.osvcurriculum.com**
For weekly scripture readings and seasonal resources

Activity

Live Your Faith

Write Family Rules Discuss the Ten Commandments, the Great Commandment, and the law of love.

- What are some ways you can add these laws to your family's rules?

- Write a list of family rules to help everyone live together in peace, love, and unity.

- Hang the list where everyone can see it.

Family Rules
1.
2.
3.
4.
5.
Jeff
Sue
Mom
Dad

People of Faith

Saint Teresa Margaret Redi went to school in a convent in Florence, Italy, from the time she was nine years old. She saw God's love in all things. She could not believe that others did not know how much God loved them. Saint Teresa Margaret worked with the sick and had a gift for healing. Her favorite phrase was "God is love." Her feast day is March 7.

▲ Teresa Margaret Redi, 1747–1770

Family Prayer

Saint Teresa, pray for us that we may love God and others with all our hearts. Amen.

© Our Sunday Visitor Curriculum Division

Chapter 8 Making Good Choices

Let Us Pray

Leader: Lord, help us to make good choices.

"I will instruct you and show you
the way you should walk."

Psalm 32:8

All: Lord, help us to make good choices. Amen.

 **Activity** Let's Begin

New Friends Paul and Tony moved to a new town on the same day. They played together all summer. They couldn't wait to start school. Paul and Tony were thrilled that they would be in class together.

On the first day Tony and Paul ate lunch together. Then they went outside to play. Sam came over to ask Tony to play kickball with some of the other kids. Tony said, "Yes." Then he ran off to play in the game.

Paul was very sad.

• What do you think about what Tony did?

An Unloving Choice

 **Focus** What did Jesus ask
Peter to do?

Paul remembered that sometimes it was
hard for Jesus' friends to do what was
right. Here is a story about Peter, one of
Jesus' closest friends.

✝ **SCRIPTURE** John 18:17–18, 25–27

Peter Denies Jesus

On the night before Jesus died on the
cross, soldiers came to take Jesus away.
Peter followed the soldiers and Jesus to
a courtyard. The gatekeeper said to
Peter, "You are not one of this man's
disciples, are you?" He said, "I am not."

Later Peter was standing around a
fire to keep warm. And someone
said to him, "You are not one of
his disciples, are you?" Peter said,
"I am not."

One of the slaves said, "Didn't I
see you in the garden with him?"
Again Peter said no.

From John 18:17–18, 25–27

❓ **Why was it hard for Peter to
say he was Jesus' friend?**

❓ **What do you think Jesus will
say to Peter?**

102

Jesus Forgives

Peter did not tell the truth about being Jesus' follower. He did not show his love for Jesus. After Jesus was raised from the dead, he spoke to Peter.

Three times Jesus asked Peter if he loved him. Three times Peter said yes. Jesus believed Peter and asked him to take care of his followers.

Jesus forgave Peter because Peter was sorry for what he had done. If you show that you are sorry for the wrong you do, God will forgive you.

Activity — Share Your Faith

Think: How do you show you are sorry for something?

Share: Talk about ways to show you are sorry.

Act: Next time someone tells you they are sorry, show them forgiveness.

Free to Choose

 How can you know what is right and what is wrong?

God helps you choose what is good. He gives you a **conscience**. Conscience is God's gift that helps you know right from wrong. It helps you choose what is good and turn away from sin. The Holy Spirit guides you to listen to your conscience.

Sin is a free choice to do what you know is wrong. Accidents and mistakes are not sins. A sin is something you do on purpose even though you know it is wrong. Sin hurts your friendship with God and others.

Different Choices

You know something is right when it follows God's law. You know it is wrong when it goes against the law of love.

❓ **What are some choices people your age have to make every day?**

❓ **Which of these choices are between doing right and doing wrong?**

Kinds of Sins

Some choices lead to serious sins called **mortal sins**. A mortal sin is a free choice to turn completely away from God's love, choosing to be totally cut off from God's own life.

Less serious sins are called **venial sins**. Venial sins do not completely remove a person from God's life and love. They still matter, though. They can lead to more serious sins.

God's love is always greater than sin. His mercy never ends. When you are sorry for sin, you can always ask God for forgiveness.

Words of Faith

Conscience is a gift from God that helps you know right from wrong.

Mortal sins are serious sins that cut people off from God's life.

Venial sins are less serious sins.

Activity Connect Your Faith

Read These Stories Think about each person's actions. Did the person choose to do something he or she knew was wrong?

Marita bumped into the rug and spilled the spaghetti sauce. The rug has a big red stain.

Rachel tripped Arnie, just to get even.

Asking Prayer

 **Let Us Pray**

Gather and begin with the Sign of the Cross.

Leader: Our Father, thank you for helping us find the way to life with you and peace with others.

Reader 1: You gave us the Ten Commandments to guide us in our choices.

All: Show us the way, O Lord.

Reader 2: Jesus shows us the way to love and seek forgiveness.

All: Show us the way, O Lord.

Reader 1: The Holy Spirit brings us peace and a forgiving heart.

All: Show us the way, O Lord.

Reader 2: Our family and friends help us choose all that is good.

All: Show us the way, O Lord. Amen.

Sing together.

Take, O take me as I am;
summon out what I shall be;
set your seal upon my
heart and live in me.

"Take, O Take Me As I Am" © 1994,
Iona Community, GIA Publications, Inc., agent

© Our Sunday Visitor Curriculum Division

Review and Apply

A **Work with Words** Circle the correct answer.

1. _____ helps you know right from wrong.

   Sin   **Conscience**

2. _____ is a free choice to do what you know is wrong.

   An accident   **A sin**

3. _____ sin is freely choosing to turn completely away from God's love.

   Mortal   **Venial**

4. _____ sin does not completely remove a person from God's life and love.

   Mortal   **Venial**

5. You must be _____ for your sins before you can ask God's forgiveness.

   sorry   **scared**

B **Check Understanding** Complete the sentence.
An accident is not a sin because

_____

- -

_____ .

Activity **Live Your Faith**

Draw a Picture Show someone in your family choosing to love God by following his laws.

Family Faith

Catholics Believe

- Conscience is God's gift that helps you know right from wrong.

- Sin is a free choice to do what you know is wrong.

✝ SCRIPTURE

John 21:15–19 tells the story of Peter stating his love for Jesus.

 GO online www.osvcurriculum.com
For weekly scripture readings and seasonal resources

Activity

Live Your Faith

Act Out Stories As a family, act out story lines such as spilling juice, lying about homework, and taking money without asking.

- Discuss whether the story is about an accident or a sin, and help one another understand the difference.

- Discuss how sins cause harm to oneself and others in the family.

People of Faith

Pierre was a Haitian born into slavery. Jean Berard taught him to read and write. When the Berards moved to New York City, they brought Pierre with them. Pierre became a barber. Madame Berard freed Pierre in 1807, and he helped many people. He and his wife Juliette raised his niece. Toussaint attended daily Mass. He is buried in the crypt of St. Patrick's Cathedral. In 1996 John Paul II declared Pierre "Venerable."

▲ **Venerable Pierre Toussaint, 1766–1853**

Family Prayer

Dear God, help us be generous and loving in our choices. Help us put you first in our lives. Amen.

In Unit 3 your child is learning about JESUS CHRIST.

9 God's Mercy

Let Us Pray

Leader: Blessed be our loving God of Mercy.

"You, Lord, are a merciful and gracious God,
slow to anger, most loving and true."

Psalm 86:15

All: Blessed be our loving God of Mercy. Amen.

Activity — Let's Begin

Kim's Problem Kim liked to play ball. Her mom told her to play in the park, but the park was full of big kids. Kim and Jason went to the lot next to her house to play.

Jason pitched the ball, and Kim hit it hard. The ball sailed far into the air! Kim ran to first base. Then she heard glass shatter. The ball had hit the kitchen window.

Kim knew her mom would come outside soon.

• What would you tell Kim to do?

God's Loving Kindness

 **Focus** **What does Jesus teach about forgiveness?**

© Our Sunday Visitor Curriculum Division

Faith Fact

Jesus called God Abba, which means "Father."

Breaking the window was an accident. But Kim disobeyed her mother when she went to the lot. She needs to say, "I am sorry." Jesus wanted people to know that God is always ready to forgive them when they are truly sorry.

 **SCRIPTURE** Luke 15:11–32

The Forgiving Father

Once a father had two sons. The younger son did not want to stay home. "Give me my half of your money," the son said.

The father sadly gave the younger son the money. The son went to a city far away. He wasted all his money.

The son needed more money, so he got a job feeding pigs. He did not like his job. He was sad and cold and all alone.

He said, "I will go home to my father. I will beg him to give me a job as his servant." The son started to walk home.

One day, the father saw his son far away. The father ran to meet him. The son fell into his arms and cried, "I am sorry I have sinned. I am not good enough to be your son."

The father hugged his son. He threw a big party. The older son said, "That's not fair. He disobeyed you!" But the father said, "He has come home. We must welcome him."

Based on Luke 15:11–32

❓ **How do you think the younger son felt?**

Activity — Share Your Faith

Think: Why did the father forgive his younger son?

Share: Talk about ways the father in the story is like God.

Act: Uncover a message about the story.

# = A	^ = D	* = E	% = F	+ = G	> = I
& = O	{ = R	~ = S	< = V	@ = W	

___ ___
@   *

___ ___ ___ ___ ___ ___ ___
%   &   {   +   >   <   *

___ ___   ___ ___ ___
~   +   &   ^

___ ___ ___ ___ ___ ___ ___ ___.
%   &   {   +   >   <   *   ~

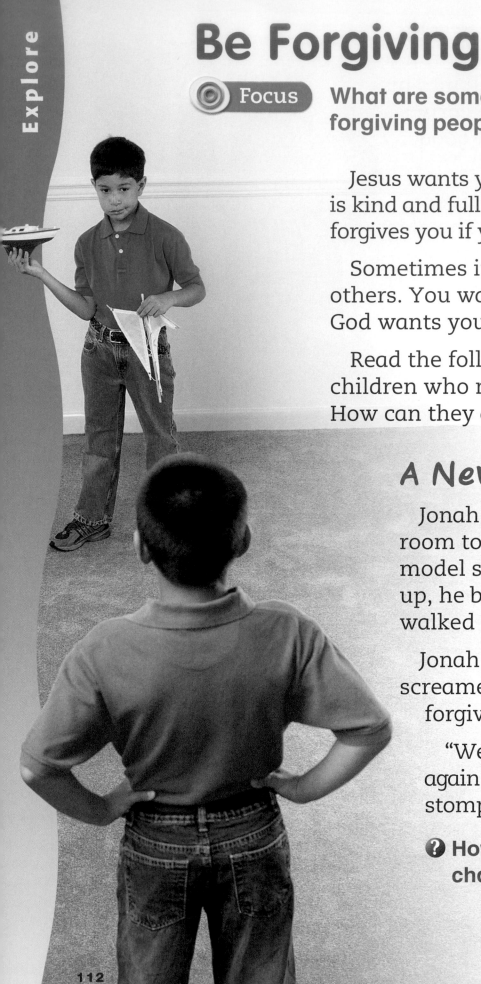

Be Forgiving

◎ Focus **What are some things that forgiving people do?**

Jesus wants you to know that God is kind and full of **mercy**. He always forgives you if you are truly sorry.

Sometimes it is not easy to forgive others. You want to stay angry. But God wants you to forgive.

Read the following stories about children who made wrong choices. How can they ask for forgiveness?

A New Model

Jonah crept into Sam's room to see his brother's new model ship. As he picked it up, he broke the sail. Sam walked in and became angry.

Jonah apologized, but Sam screamed, "I will never forgive you!"

"Well, I'll never talk to you again," said Jonah, as he stomped out of the room.

❓ How would you change this scene?

Putting Things Away

Tomoko was supposed to put the balls away after recess. She forgot. The next day the balls were gone. Tomoko told the teacher that it had been José's turn to put the balls away. José got in trouble because of Tomoko's lie.

❓ **What you would do if you were José?**

Words of Faith

Mercy is loving kindness and forgiveness.

Forgiveness

Jesus wants you to ask forgiveness when you have done wrong. And Jesus asks you to be a forgiving person, too.

Activity   Connect Your Faith

✏️ **Write a Story** With a partner, make up another story about forgiveness. Share it with your friends.

Once upon a time

Prayer for Mercy

 **Let Us Pray**

Gather and begin with the Sign of the Cross.

Sing your response to each asking prayer.

Leader: For the times when we were slow to forgive those who hurt us,

All: Lord, have mercy.

Leader: For the times when our words and actions have hurt others,

All: Christ, have mercy.

Leader: For the times when we have not told the truth,

All: Lord, have mercy.

Leader: May God give us mercy and forgiveness.

All: Amen.

Sing together.

Lord, have mercy.
  Lord, have mercy.
Christ, have mercy.
  Christ, have mercy.
Lord, have mercy.
Lord, have mercy.

"Kyrie Eleison" © 1973, ICEL.

CHAPTER 9

Review and Apply

Work With Words Fill in the blank with the correct word from the Word Bank.

WORD BANK

Jesus
sorry
forgive
mercy
forgiving

1. God is always ready to

_____

_____ you.

2. God is kind and full of

_____

_____ .

3. God will forgive you if you are truly

_____

_____ .

_____

4. _____ asks you to forgive others as God forgives you.

5. You show mercy when you are

_____

_____ .

Activity   Live Your Faith

Make a Friendship Bracelet If a friend has hurt you and is sorry, give the bracelet to show your forgiveness.

Make another bracelet for yourself. Call it a reminder bracelet. It can remind you to be kind and forgiving toward everyone.

Family Faith

Catholics Believe

■ God is merciful and forgiving.

■ God will always forgive you if you are truly sorry.

SCRIPTURE

Read Psalm 145:8–13 to praise God for his mercy.

GO online www.osvcurriculum.com
For weekly scripture readings and seasonal resources

Activity

Live Your Faith

Forgiveness Role-Plays In what special ways do you ask for and offer forgiveness? Think about peaceful words to say when offering forgiveness to each other. Role-play

• telling someone you are sorry
• asking for forgiveness
• accepting an apology
• giving forgiveness

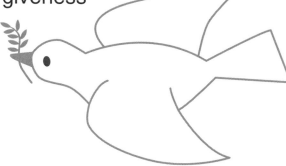

People of Faith

▲ Blessed Pope John Paul II, 1920–2005

Pope John Paul II traveled around the world telling everyone about God's love and mercy. One day, a man tried to kill the pope. The pope was rushed to the hospital. When the pope was well, he went to the prison to visit the man who shot him. John Paul II forgave the man. The pope's actions remind everyone that God's mercy is for everyone. John Paul II was beatified in 2011.

Family Prayer

God our Father, thank you for Blessed Pope John Paul II. Help us be merciful and forgiving. Amen.

In Unit 3 your child is learning about JESUS CHRIST.

Unit 3 Review

Work with Words Use the clues to find the words in the word search. Circle each word when you find it.

```
c  o  m  m  a  n  d  m  e  n  t  s
o  a  e  e  c  p  r  z  o  s  t  m
n  f  s  r  c  z  s  l  j  p  r  o
s  a  b  c  i  o  p  o  e  a  b  r
c  q  n  y  d  d  z  v  s  q  c  t
i  w  g  t  e  h  r  e  u  m  o  a
e  f  r  g  n  v  z  a  s  y  h  l
n  z  s  m  t  a  o  b  e  d  c  a
c  p  i  e  f  c  v  e  n  i  a  l
e  x  n  y  f  o  r  g  i  v  e  s
```

1. God's laws

2. The free choice to disobey God

3. What God does if you are sorry

4. Sin that does not completely remove you from God's grace

5. Very serious sin

6. Loving forgiveness and kindness

7. Jesus teaches us to do this

8. This is not a sin

9. This helps you know right from wrong

10. He gave the law of love

Unit 4
The Church

In this unit you will...

learn that God shares his life with the Church. Grace is sharing in God's life. The sacraments are signs and celebrations of God's life. They give us grace. They help us celebrate our friendship with Jesus. They help us follow Jesus. The Church year celebrates the life, death and Resurrection of Jesus.

Chapter
10

Chapter
11

Chapter
12

What do you think you will learn in this unit about the Church?

118

Chapter 10 Signs of Love

 **Let Us Pray**

Leader: God, thank you for sharing your life with us.

"Come and see the works of God,
awesome in the deeds done for us."

Psalm 66:5

All: God, thank you for sharing your life with us. Amen.

Activity — Let's Begin

My Abuela and Me Some weekends I visit my grandmother. I call her *Abuela*. She meets me at school on Friday, and gives me a big hug. Then we take the subway to her apartment.

Abuela makes my favorite foods and plays games with me. She listens to me and takes care of me. Sometimes Abuela leaves me a note in my book bag. This is another sign of her love for me.

• What are the signs of love in this story?

Jesus Shares Life

Focus What are the sacraments?

Jesus' actions were signs of love that brought people closer to God. Jesus welcomed people who felt alone. He fed people who were hungry. Jesus forgave and healed people. In these ways Jesus shared God's life with others.

Jesus asked his disciples to continue sharing his love. The Holy Spirit gave the disciples the power to do what Jesus had done.

Faith Fact

People of any age can be baptized.

✝ **SCRIPTURE**   Acts 8:4–12

People Everywhere Believe

Philip traveled to different towns to tell others the good news about Jesus. He shared Jesus' message and love and even healed people who were sick. Many people began to believe in Jesus and were baptized.

Based on Acts 8:4–12

❓ **Why did the people ask to be baptized?**

Holy Signs

The Catholic Church shares God's life and love through special celebrations called sacraments. A **sacrament** is a holy sign that comes from Jesus and gives God's life. This sharing in God's life is called **grace**.

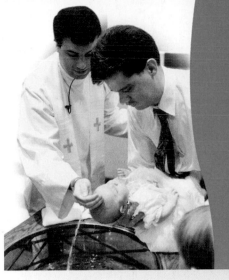

Baptism is the first sacrament a person receives. Through Baptism a person is given new life in Christ. He or she becomes a child of God and member of the Church.

In the celebration of Baptism, a priest or deacon pours water over the head of the person being baptized and says, "I baptize you in the name of the Father, and of the Son, and of the Holy Spirit." The person receives a lit candle as a sign of walking in the light of Jesus.

Words of Faith

A **sacrament** is a holy sign that comes from Jesus and gives life.

Grace is sharing in God's life.

❓ **What do you know about your own Baptism?**

Activity — Share Your Faith

Think: What are some ways you can walk in the light of Jesus?

Share: Share your thoughts with a small group.

✏ **Act:** Write one thing you will do to follow Jesus this week.

_____

_____

_____

_____

The Seven Sacraments

Baptism

Confirmation

Eucharist

Reconciliation

Anointing of the Sick

Matrimony

Holy Orders

Focus How do people become members of the Church?

The sacraments give new life, healing, nourishment, and a share in the work of Jesus. There are seven sacraments.

The sacraments celebrate Jesus' presence among his people. When you receive the sacraments, you grow in your love for God and others. God's life in you grows stronger.

❓ What sacraments have you seen celebrated?

❓ What sacraments will you receive soon?

The Sacraments of Initiation

Baptism, Confirmation, and Eucharist are the Sacraments of Initiation. *Initiation* means "beginning." These sacraments welcome new members into the Church.

Through Baptism a person is given new life in Christ. In Confirmation the Holy Spirit strengthens people to be followers of Jesus. In the Eucharist, Jesus' Body and Blood are received.

People of any age can become members of the Catholic Church. Sometimes all three Sacraments of Initiation are received in the same celebration. This happens at the beginning of Easter. Other times the Sacraments are spread out over many years. Everyone is invited to follow Jesus and join the Church.

Activity — Connect Your Faith

Welcome New Members What do you think new Catholics need to know about Christ and the Church? Make a welcome card and bring it to your parish for someone who has just become a Catholic.

Welcome

Prayer for Gathering

 **Let Us Pray**

Gather and begin with the Sign of the Cross.

Leader: Blessed be the name of the Lord.

All: Now and forever.

Reader: A reading from the First Letter of Paul to the Corinthians.

Read 1 Corinthians 12:12.

The word of the Lord.

All: Thanks be to God.

Leader: Let us pray.

Bow your heads as the leader prays.

All: Amen.

Sing together the refrain.

We come to share our story,
we come to break the bread.

We come to know our rising
from the dead.

"Song of the Body of Christ/Canción del
Cuerpo de Cristo" © 1989, GIA Publications, Inc.

Review and Apply

A **Work with Words** Write the letter of the correct word or words from the Word Bank to complete each sentence.

WORD BANK
a. sacrament
b. Holy Spirit
c. candle
d. grace
e. Initiation

1. Baptism and Eucharist are sacraments of _____.

2. At Baptism, a _____ is given to show the light of Jesus.

3. In Confirmation, you are made stronger by the _____.

4. A _____ is a holy sign that comes from Jesus.

5. Sharing in God's life is called _____.

B **Check Understanding** Write your answer on the lines. What happens in baptism?

_____

_ _

_____

_ _

_____

Activity Live Your Faith

Show Others God When you were baptized, you were given God's new life. Write one way you can help others see God.

_____

_ _

_____

_ _

Family Faith

Catholics Believe

- Grace is sharing in God's life.

- Sacraments are holy signs that come from Jesus and give grace.

✝ SCRIPTURE

Read Mark 14:22–25 about the first Eucharist at the Last Supper.

GO online www.osvcurriculum.com
For weekly scripture readings and seasonal resources

Live Your Faith

Look Back Discuss the Sacraments of Initiation. Recall these special days with your children by sharing pictures and videos. Talk about how your family celebrates special days. Have family members choose favorite photos and stories to include in a scrapbook about one sacrament.

People of Faith

▲ Saint John Berchmans, 1599–1621

John was a prayerful, friendly and cheerful person. He was about to become a priest when he died suddenly. John was known for his love of prayer and his work as an altar boy. When he was only 7, he would sometimes serve at 2 or 3 masses a day. People remembered how prayerful John was and how he loved the celebration of Eucharist. For this reason, John was named the patron saint of altar servers. His feast day is August 13.

Family Prayer

Saint John, pray for us that we may always show respect and joy as we celebrate the sacraments. Amen.

In Unit 4 your child is learning about the ch r ch.

The Church and Forgiveness

Let Us Pray

Leader: Thank you, God, for your forgiveness.
"Lord, you are kind and forgiving,
    most loving to all who call on you."

Psalm 86:5

All: Thank you, God, for your forgiveness. Amen.

Activity Let's Begin

New Again Jared has a little brother named Benny. Benny had a special teddy bear named Fuzzy. Benny loved Fuzzy so much that all his fuzz came off. One of Fuzzy's legs tore open, and his stuffing began to fall out.

Jared went to his aunt for help. Benny stood by and watched her sew up Fuzzy. Soon he was as good as he could be. Benny was as happy as he could be, too.

• Tell another story about a thing that was broken and had to be fixed.

Repairing Hurts

 **Focus** How can you show you are sorry and ask for forgiveness?

Benny's aunt fixed Fuzzy's torn leg. How do you fix the hurts that you cause? In this story, Jesus shows you how.

✝ **SCRIPTURE** Luke 7:36–39, 48–50

The Woman Who Was Sorry

One day, Jesus was having dinner. An uninvited woman came into the room. The woman knelt at the feet of Jesus. She was sorry for her sins. Her tears fell on Jesus' feet. Then she dried his feet with her long hair. After that she poured sweet-smelling oil on his feet.

Jesus spoke up for the woman. "She has bathed [my feet] with her tears and . . . anointed my feet with ointment. So I tell you, her many sins have been forgiven; hence, she has shown great love."

Then Jesus said to the woman, "Your sins are forgiven . . . Your faith has saved you; go in peace."

Based on Luke 7:36–39, 48–50

❓ **How did the woman show she was sorry for her sins?**

❓ **How do you show you are sorry?**

Examination of Conscience

There are times you may choose not to obey God's laws. This hurts your friendship with God and others.

You can ask the Holy Spirit to help you see where you have made wrong choices. You can think about your thoughts, words, and actions. This prayerful way of looking at your life is called an examination of conscience. These are a few questions that will help you.

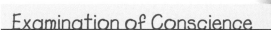

Examination of Conscience

1. Did you put God first in your life?

2. Did you use God's name in a holy way?

3. Did you keep Sunday a holy day?

4. Did you obey your parents and teachers?

5. Did you hurt another person on purpose?

After you think about your sins, you can tell God that you are sorry. Then tell him you will try harder to live by his commandments. This means you have **contrition** for your sins.

Words of Faith

Contrition is being sorry for sin and wanting to live better.

Activity — Share Your Faith

Think: What is another question you can ask yourself during an examination of conscience?

Share: Talk about some questions with a partner.

Act: Write two questions on a separate piece of paper.

129

The Sacrament of Reconciliation

 **Focus** How does the Church celebrate God's forgiveness?

After examining your conscience and being sorry for your sins, you are ready to celebrate the Church's Sacrament of Forgiveness. This sacrament is also called the **Sacrament of Reconciliation**, or the Sacrament of Penance. Each time you receive the sacrament, you receive God's forgiveness and celebrate your friendship with God.

You can receive the Sacrament of Reconciliation individually or as part of a parish celebration. These are the steps to celebrate the Sacrament of Reconciliation individually. The priest will help you if you forget a step.

❓ When does your parish celebrate this sacrament?

Steps in the Sacrament

1. **Welcome Rites** The priest greets you with the Sign of the Cross.

2. **Scripture Reading** The priest reads, or you quietly read, a Bible passage about forgiveness.

3. **Confession and Penance** You tell your sins to the priest, who can never tell anyone your sins. He talks with you about ways you can do better. He gives you a **penance**.

4. **Contrition** You pray an Act of Contrition.

5. **Absolution** The priest forgives, or absolves, your sins in the name of the Father, the Son, and the Holy Spirit.

6. **Closing** The priest prays, "Give thanks to the Lord, for he is good." You say, "His mercy endures forever." You go out to do better and to make up for what you have done wrong.

© Our Sunday Visitor Curriculum Division

Words of Faith

In the **Sacrament of Reconciliation** God's forgiveness for sin is given through the Church.

A **penance** is a prayer or an act to make up for sin.

Absolution is the forgiveness of sin you receive from God through the Church in the Sacrament of Reconciliation.

Activity   Connect Your Faith

Show Good Actions

Show a child doing good actions after receiving the Sacrament of Reconciliation.

Prayer for Forgiveness

 **Let Us Pray**

Gather and begin with the Sign of the Cross.

Leader: God our Father, be with us now as we think about ways we can be better.

Sing together.

It's me, it's me, Oh Lord,
Standin' in the need of prayer.
It's me, it's me, Oh Lord,
Standin' in the need of prayer.

"Standin' in the Need of Prayer" African-American Spiritual

Group 1: We have not been as helpful as we could be.

All: But you love and come to us.

Group 2: We have not been as kind to others as we could be.

All: But you love and come to us.

Leader: Let us give thanks for God's forgiveness and pray the Act of Contrition.

Based on Rite of Penance

Review and Apply

A **Check Understanding** Use the numbers 1 through 6. Put the steps of the celebration of the Sacrament of Reconciliation in order.

Step _____ I listen to a story of forgiveness.

Step _____ The priest greets me with the Sign of the Cross.

Step _____ I tell my sins to the priest.

Step _____ The priest forgives my sins.

Step _____ I pray an Act of Contrition.

Step _____ I try to do better.

B **Make Connections** Complete the sentence.

The Sacrament of Reconciliation celebrates

_____

_____

_____

_____

_____ .

Activity Live Your Faith

Describe Reconciliation Imagine that you receive an e-mail from a friend asking about the Sacrament of Reconciliation. Write back and describe the celebration of Reconciliation in your own words. Use a separate piece of paper.

Family Faith

⊙ Catholics Believe

- In the Sacrament of Reconciliation you receive God's forgiveness.

- The sacrament also celebrates your friendship with God and the Church.

✝ SCRIPTURE

Jesus' parable of the unforgiving servant (Matthew 18:21–35) is about forgiving others.

 www.osvcurriculum.com
For weekly scripture readings and seasonal resources

Activity
Live Your Faith

Examine Your Conscience As part of the family evening ritual, take some time to think about events of the day.

- Work together to develop questions to help each person examine his or her conscience.
- Allow time for each person to silently ask God for forgiveness.
- Pray together an Act of Contrition.

People of Faith

Paul did not like Christians. He helped put them in jail. One day, Paul heard Jesus say, "Why do you persecute me?" Paul realized that he had done wrong. That very minute, Paul stopped hurting Christians. Instead, he went everywhere telling people about Jesus, his Lord and Savior. Many people became followers of Jesus because of Paul's work. Paul was put in jail for believing in Jesus. The feast day of Saint Paul is July 25.

▲ Saint Paul, first century

Family Prayer

Saint Paul, pray for us that we may follow Jesus and change for the better. Lead us to Jesus, our Lord and Savior. Amen.

© Our Sunday Visitor Curriculum Division

In Unit 4 your child is learning about the ch r ch.

Chapter 12 The Church Year

Let Us Pray

Leader: Lord, we praise you every day.

"Only goodness and love will pursue me
all the days of my life." Psalm 23:6

All: Lord, we praise you every day. Amen.

Activity Let's Begin

Puzzling Questions

Dear Mr. Sun,

Why is it dark in the morning when I go to school in winter? Why is it light in the morning when I can sleep late in the summer?

Why is it so hot in summer that I have to go for a swim? Why is it so cool in fall that I must wear a jacket?

Why do you melt the snow in winter? Why don't you melt the flowers in spring?

Thank you for shining so brightly most days where I live.

Your friend,
Josie Luna

• What are some things about the seasons of the year that puzzle you?

The Church's Seasons

 **Focus** What is celebrated in the Church year?

During the year the Church's **liturgy** celebrates the events in the life of Jesus. The Church celebrates the light of Jesus throughout the Church year.

✝ **SCRIPTURE**

Jesus spoke to his followers saying, "I am the light of the world. Whoever follows me will not walk in darkness, but will have the light of life."

John 8:12

During the four weeks of Advent, the Church gets ready to celebrate Jesus' birth. You tell God that you want to get better at loving him and others. Just as the seasons have different colors, so do the Church's seasons. The color for Advent is violet. It is a sign of getting ready and change of heart.

The pink candle is for joy that Christmas is almost here.

Why is only one candle pink in the Advent wreath?

Christmas

The three weeks of the Christmas Season celebrate Jesus' presence in the world. The Son of God came so all people could know his Father's love. The Christmas celebrations help people love Jesus and other people more. White is the color for the Christmas Season. It is a sign of great joy.

Ordinary Time

Ordinary Time comes twice during the Church year. The first time is after the Christmas Season. The second is after the Easter Season. During these times you learn more about Jesus and grow as his follower. Green is the season's color because it is the color of growth.

Words of Faith

The **liturgy** is the public worship of the Church. It includes the sacraments and forms of daily prayer.

Activity — Share Your Faith

Think: What seasons of the Church year do you know?

Share: Talk about the seasons. How are they alike? How are they different? What season is the Church in now?

Act: Write about a Church season you really like to celebrate.

The Greatest Celebration

Focus What is the greatest feast of the Church year?

The Season of Lent is a preparation for the important feast of Easter. For forty days and six Sundays, the Church's color is violet. As during Advent, you are asked to make changes that will help you grow closer to Jesus. You are to pray more often and help others.

We do special things for Jesus during Lent.

The Three Days

What good things can I do?

The three days before Easter are the holiest days of the Church year. On Holy Thursday the Church celebrates Jesus' gift of the Eucharist at the Last Supper. It is a joyous occasion, so the color is white.

On Good Friday the Church gives thanks to Jesus as Savior. The color is red because Jesus died for all people.

Holy Saturday evening begins the Easter celebration. For this joyous feast, the color is white.

Easter

Every Sunday the Church celebrates the **Resurrection**, when Jesus was raised from the dead. But each year, the Church celebrates the Resurrection of Jesus for fifty days from Easter to Pentecost. Easter is the greatest feast of the Church year. The color during this season is white.

The last ten days of this season celebrate Jesus' promise to send the Holy Spirit. Pentecost is the celebration of the Holy Spirit coming to the Apostles. For this feast the color red is used as a sign of the power of the Holy Spirit.

❓ **Why do you think Easter is the greatest feast of the Church year?**

© Our Sunday Visitor Curriculum Division

Words of Faith

The **Resurrection** is the mystery of Jesus being raised from death.

Activity Connect Your Faith

Find the Hidden Word Color the X's yellow and O's blue and red to discover the Easter word.

139

Prayer of Praise

 **Let Us Pray**

Gather and begin with the Sign of the Cross.

Leader: God our Father, we thank you for all that is beautiful in the world and for the happiness you give us.

Reader 1: We praise you for your daylight and for your word which gives light to our minds.

Reader 2: We praise you for the earth and all the people on it.

All: We know that you are good. You love us and do great things for us.

From EP for Children, #1

Sing together the refrain.

Dance, then, wherever you
  may be,

I am the Lord of the Dance,
  said he,

And I'll lead you all, wherever you may be,

And I'll lead you all in the Dance, said he.

"I Danced in the Morning" © 1963 Stainer & Bell Ltd.

Review and Apply

A Check Understanding Match the description of the season in Column I with the letter of the correct season in Column 2.

Column I	Column 2
1. Three weeks of joy that celebrate Jesus' presence in the world. _____	**a.** Advent
2. This season comes twice during the year. _____	**b.** Christmas
3. Four weeks of getting ready to celebrate Jesus' birth. _____	**c.** Lent
4. The greatest feast of the year that celebrates Jesus' Resurrection. _____	**d.** Ordinary Time
5. Forty days of praying and helping others as a way to prepare for Easter. _____	**e.** Easter

B Make Connections Write your answer on the lines. What is the Church year?

_____

- - - - - - - - - - - - - - - - - - -

_____

_____

- - - - - - - - - - - - - - - - - - -

_____

Activity Live Your Faith

Listen to Readings Listen as your teacher reads the Gospel story for Sunday Mass. What did you learn from this story? What do you think Jesus wants you to do? Share your ideas.

Family Faith

Catholics Believe

- The Church year celebrates the life, death, and Resurrection of Jesus.

- The Resurrection is the mystery of Jesus being raised from death.

✝ SCRIPTURE

Read Ecclesiastes 3:1–8 to find out what God says about time.

GO online www.osvcurriculum.com
For weekly scripture readings and seasonal resources

Activity

Live Your Faith

Make a Poster Look around your church. Talk about the colors and signs of the Church season that is being celebrated now. Work together to make a poster of the Church season to display in your home.

People of Faith

Pope Saint Victor was one of three popes from Africa. He decided with the bishops that Easter must be celebrated on Sunday. Saint Victor also declared that the Mass should be celebrated in the language of the people. At that time the language was Latin. The Church celebrates his feast day on July 28.

▲ **Pope Saint Victor,** 197–199 A.D.

Family Prayer

Pope Saint Victor, ask God to help us bring his message to our friends and family. Amen.

In Unit 4 your child is learning about the ch r ch.

Unit 4 Review

A **Work with Words** Complete each sentence with the correct word from the Word Bank.

WORD BANK

Sacrament
Grace
Liturgy
Absolution
Contrition

1. _____ is the public worship of the church.

2. A _____ is a holy sign that comes from Jesus and gives us life.

3. _____ is being sorry for sin and wanting to live better.

4. _____ is sharing in God's life.

5. _____ is the forgiveness of sin from God in the Sacrament of Reconciliation.

B **Check Understanding** Circle the correct answer.

6. What does the word Resurrection mean?

   Jesus died   Jesus was born   Jesus rose from death

7. What does Pentecost celebrate?

   death of Jesus   life of Jesus   coming of Holy Spirit

8. What is the first sacrament you receive?

   Confirmation   Eucharist   Baptism

9. What sacrament celebrates God's forgiveness?

   Anointing   Reconciliation   Eucharist

10. What does Christmas celebrate?

    death of Jesus   life of Jesus   birth of Jesus

143

Unit 5
Morality

In this unit you will...

learn that Jesus told us that the kingdom of God is where we discover love, peace and justice. All are welcome in the kingdom. We are Jesus' followers. He taught us how to pray. We share in his life and work. We share the good news with the world. We pray, we forgive, and we love.

Chapter 13

Chapter 14

Chapter 15

What do you think you will learn in this unit about being a follower of Jesus?

Chapter 13 Care for All People

Let Us Pray

Leader: Lord, we praise you for your love.

"Your love for me is great."

Psalm 86:13

All: Lord, we praise you for your love. Amen.

Activity Let's Begin

Come In "Will she know me? What will she say?" I wondered as I knocked on the principal's door.

"What a surprise! Hello, Omar, welcome to my office."

I handed the principal the note to leave early.

"Have a good time with your grandmother this afternoon, Omar. We'll miss you."

• When have you felt welcome? With a partner, act out the scene.

Jesus' Example

 **Focus** How did Zacchaeus show his faith in God?

The principal made Omar feel welcome. Here is a time that Jesus showed that God welcomes everyone.

✝ SCRIPTURE

Luke 19:1–8

A Surprise Guest

Word went out uphill and down,
Jesus was coming to Jericho town.

Zacchaeus, you know, was too short to see,
So he scurried right up a sycamore tree.

"Zacchaeus, come down, come down, I say.
Let's have dinner at your house today."

Jesus and Zacchaeus walked by the crowd
who grumbled and mumbled and said out loud:

"He is a sinner and he is a snitch.
He took our money. That's why he is rich."

Zacchaeus proclaimed in a loud, clear tone,
"To the poor I will give half of all that I own."

146

Then Jesus said, "God's love has no end.
My friend, Zacchaeus, is also God's friend.

Put away your frowns. Be full of cheer.
God's love and kindness are truly here.

God calls everyone, the
   small and the great.

So, come gather around.
   Come celebrate!"

Based on Luke 19:1–8

Words of Faith

Faith is belief in God and all that he has told about himself.

❓ **What did the mumblers and grumblers say?**

❓ **What did Jesus say?**

The Surprise Ending

Jesus saw that Zacchaeus had **faith** in God. Zacchaeus wanted to follow Jesus. So Jesus surprised all. He welcomed Zacchaeus to share in God's love.

Activity — Share Your Faith

Think: Imagine that Jesus has come to your house. What would you say and do?

_____

_____

_____

_____

_____

Share: Tell a partner how you would feel.

Act: Take turns role playing this with your partner.

All Are Welcome

◎ Focus Who does Jesus invite to God's kingdom?

It did not matter to Jesus how old a person was or how tall. Jesus welcomed everyone to talk with him.

✝ SCRIPTURE   Matthew 19:13–15

Little Children

People often brought their children to Jesus. The disciples said, "Don't bother Jesus. He is too busy!" But Jesus said, "Let the children come to me . . . for the kingdom of heaven belongs to such as these."

Jesus welcomed the children and blessed them. Then he sent the children on their way.

Based on Matthew 19:13–15

❓ How did Jesus treat the children?

In God's Kingdom

Another name for the kingdom of Heaven is the **kingdom of God**. Jesus invites everyone to enter the kingdom of love and peace. Jesus knew how to make people feel welcome. Many people came to him for help and healing. Some people were like Zacchaeus. They thought Jesus wouldn't care about them. Jesus taught that all people are welcome in God's kingdom.

Like Jesus, the Catholic Church welcomes all people. Every Sunday there are people who welcome each Church member before Mass begins. These welcomers can be men, women, or children.

❓ **How are you welcomed by others?**

© Our Sunday Visitor Curriculum Division

Words of Faith

The **kingdom of God** is love, peace, and justice for all.

Activity Connect Your Faith

✏️ **Trace Your Foot** Cut out the traced foot. Write your name on it. Using everyone's footprints, make a trail in the classroom leading to your prayer center.

Prayer of Welcome

 Let Us Pray

Gather and make the Sign of the Cross.

Leader: God our Father, we gather together in Jesus' name.

Reader 1: When we welcome a friend,

All: Jesus' love shows through us.

Reader 2: When we welcome a child who is left out,

All: Jesus' love shows through us.

Reader 3: When we take extra time to help,

All: Jesus' love shows through us.

Leader: Let us pray.

Bow your heads as the leader prays.

All: Amen.

Sing together.

Fill us with your love,
   O Lord,
   and we will sing
      for joy!

"Psalm 90: Fill Us with Your Love"
© 1969, 1981, and 1997, ICEL

Review and Apply

Work with Words Fill in the blank with the correct word or words from the Word Bank.

WORD BANK
welcomes
kingdom of God
Faith
children
Zacchaeus

1. ____________ became Jesus' friend.
2. Jesus ____________ everyone.
3. Jesus blessed the ____________.
4. Everyone is invited into the ____________.
5. ____________ is belief in God.

Activity Live Your Faith

Make a Welcome List Write what makes you feel welcome. Use these ways to welcome new friends.

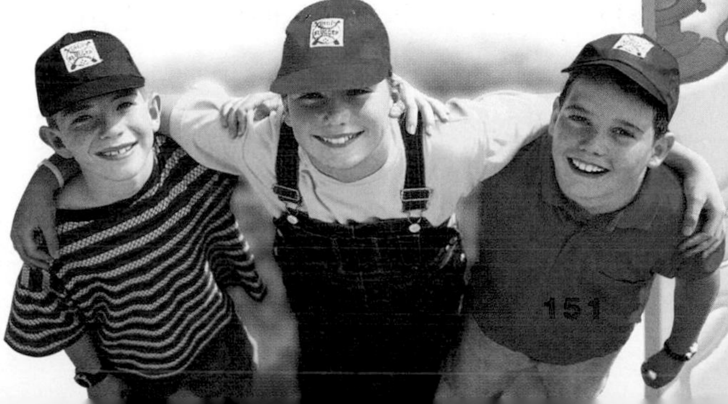

Family Faith

Catholics Believe

- The kingdom of God is love, peace, and justice for all.

- Everyone is welcome in God's kingdom and the Catholic Church.

SCRIPTURE

Matthew 18:1–5 tells of the special place of children in God's kingdom.

GO online www.osvcurriculum.com
For weekly scripture readings and seasonal resources

Live Your Faith

Do Acts of Kindness Write the name of each family member on a separate slip of paper. Put all the slips in a cup.

- Have each family member draw a name.
- For one week, each member of the family is to do small acts of kindness for the person whose name he or she drew.

People of Faith

Brigid was a nun who dedicated her life to God. Others soon joined her. Brigid went all around Ireland. She walked. She traveled by horse and cart. She sailed in a boat on the Irish Sea. Everywhere Brigid went, she spoke of the love of God. She was known for her kindness and mercy to everyone. Saint Brigid is a patron saint of Ireland. Her feast day is February 1.

▲ Saint Brigid of Kildare, d. c. 525

Family Prayer

Saint Brigid, pray for us that we may be strong and lively in the love of God. Amen.

In Unit 5 your child is learning about morality.

Chapter 14 Share the Good News

 Let Us Pray

Leader: Jesus, you are with us always.
"Christ lives in me."
Galatians 2:20

All: Jesus, you are with us always. Amen.

Activity Let's Begin

Someone Special Justin keeps stories and pictures of his uncle.

Uncle Matt is a hockey player. He can skate faster than anyone Justin knows. His uncle sets goals and works hard to reach them.

Now Uncle Matt's team is going to play in the regional finals. Justin wants everybody to know about his Uncle Matt.

• How do you tell people about someone you admire?

Live as Followers

 **Focus** **What did Jesus ask his followers to do?**

Justin wanted everyone to know about his Uncle Matt. Jesus wanted everyone to know about God his Father.

Jesus knew that the work of spreading his message would be hard. His followers would need his help. He made a promise. If they stayed close to him, they would do many good things.

✝ SCRIPTURE   John 15:4–5

The Vine and the Branches

Jesus told his disciples "Remain in me, as I remain in you. A branch cannot bear fruit unless it remains on the vine. You cannot bear fruit and do good things unless you remain in me."

Jesus said, "I am the vine, you are the branches. Whoever remains in me and I in him will bear much fruit."

From John 15:4–5

❓ **How can you stay close to Jesus?**

The Message to Others

After Jesus was raised from the dead, he gathered with his disciples. He wanted them to share in his work.

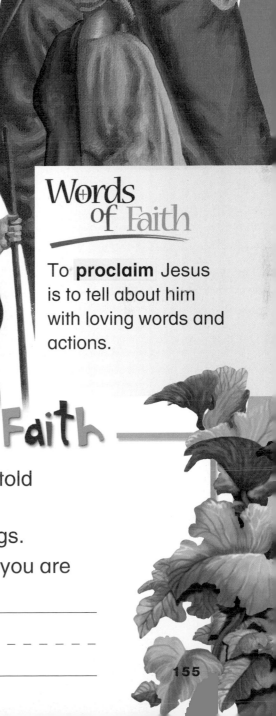

✝ SCRIPTURE

"Go, therefore, and make disciples of all nations, baptizing them in the name of the Father, and of the Son, and of the Holy Spirit, teaching them to observe all that I have commanded you. And behold I am with you always."

Matthew 28:19–20

The Holy Spirit guided Jesus' followers to places that they had never seen. The Spirit strengthened them to **proclaim** the good news. They told the people everything that Jesus had taught them.

Words of Faith

To **proclaim** Jesus is to tell about him with loving words and actions.

Activity — Share Your Faith

Think: What do you think Jesus' followers told others about him?

Share: With a partner talk about these things.

🖊 **Act:** Write one thing you can do to show you are a follower of Jesus.

_____

- - - - - - - - - - - - - - - - - - - -

_____

Jesus' Followers Today

Focus How do people share Jesus' message?

There are over 1 billion Catholics in the world.

Jesus' followers still bring his message to the world. People do this in different ways. Here are some people who serve Jesus and share his love with others.

- Sister Rosa helps children learn more about God.

- Mr. Rodriguez teaches songs so that children can sing to God.

- Parents and grandparents teach their children to pray.

© Our Sunday Visitor Curriculum Division

- Father Ed celebrates Mass and gives the people the gift of Jesus.

- Deacon Jerry helps in the parish by baptizing people.

 Draw one way someone in your parish helps.

Prayer of Thanksgiving

 **Let Us Pray**

Gather and begin with the Sign of the Cross.

Leader: We praise and thank you, O Lord for the many people who share your good news.

Blessed be the name of the Lord.

All: Now and forever.

Leader: We praise and thank you, O Lord for the people who help in our parish.

Blessed be the name of the Lord.

All: Now and forever. Amen.

Sing together.

We are sent two by two.
Sent as church in the world.
Sent to share God's
 good news,
Sing and tell, spread
 the Word.

"Two By Two" © 2000, GIA Publications, Inc.

Review and Apply

Check Understanding Circle the correct answer.

1. Jesus told his disciples to make _____ of all nations.

   friends   **slaves**   **disciples**

2. _____ was sent to help Jesus' disciples.

   God the Father   **The Holy Spirit**   **Mary his mother**

3. Jesus told his followers that he would be with them _____.

   always   **for a short time**   **for ten years**

4. Jesus told his followers to _____ and teach all nations.

   baptize   **confirm**   **shake hands**

5. Jesus is the _____ and we are the branches.

   vine   **leaves**   **soil**

Activity Live Your Faith

Make a Small Banner Write a message. Tell some Good News of Jesus. Give it to someone who needs to hear good news.

Catholics Believe

- Jesus' disciples share in his life and in his work.

- Jesus is with us always.

SCRIPTURE

Read I Corinthians 12:4–6 to learn what Saint Paul says about different ways to serve God.

GO online **www.osvcurriculum.com**
For weekly scripture readings and seasonal resources

Activity
Live Your Faith

Loving Actions As a family, choose a loving action that will be practiced by every family member for a week. Emphasize that a smile or an act of courtesy may brighten someone's day. At the end of the week, talk about how the family members feel about the loving actions.

People of Faith

A little girl named Agnes grew up to be **Mother Teresa**. She worked in India, far from her home. She cared for the poor and dying. She began a new group of sisters called the Missionaries of Charity. When people asked, "What can we do to help the people who are poor?" Mother Teresa told them to do their best for God right where they were. She said, "Do something beautiful for God." Mother Teresa was beatified by Pope John Paul II in 2003.

▲ **Blessed Mother Teresa of Calcutta, 1910–1997**

 Family Prayer

Dear Jesus, help us bear the fruit of your love. Help us do something beautiful for God, as Blessed Mother Teresa did. Amen.

In Unit 5 your child is learning about MORALITY.

Pray as Jesus Did

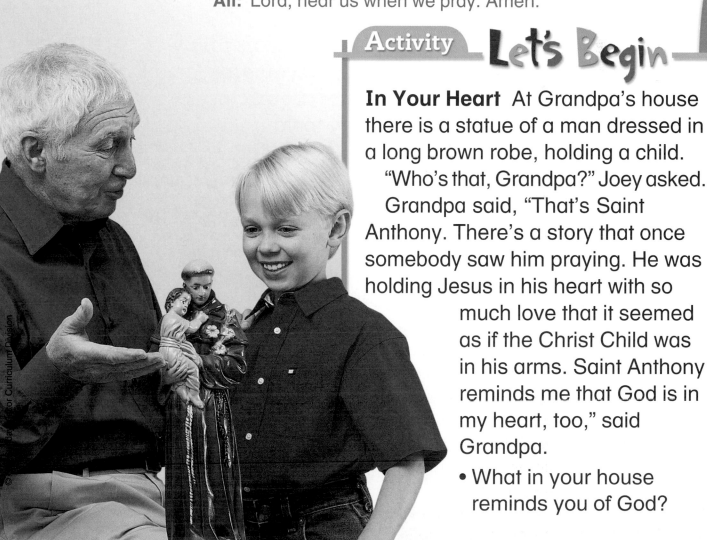

Let Us Pray

Leader: Lord, hear us when we pray.

"Gladden the soul of your servant;
to you, Lord, I lift up my soul."

Psalm 86:4

All: Lord, hear us when we pray. Amen.

Activity — Let's Begin

In Your Heart At Grandpa's house there is a statue of a man dressed in a long brown robe, holding a child.

"Who's that, Grandpa?" Joey asked. Grandpa said, "That's Saint Anthony. There's a story that once somebody saw him praying. He was holding Jesus in his heart with so much love that it seemed as if the Christ Child was in his arms. Saint Anthony reminds me that God is in my heart, too," said Grandpa.

• What in your house reminds you of God?

Time with God

 **Focus** How does Jesus want you to pray?

When you pray, you talk to and listen to God. The Bible says that Jesus prayed often. He wanted his followers to pray often, too.

 **SCRIPTURE** Matthew 6:5–9

How to Pray

Jesus told his followers, "When you pray, go to your inner room, close the door, and pray to your Father in secret."

Jesus also told them, "Do not babble like the others, who think that they will be heard because of their many words . . . Your Father knows what you need before you ask him. This is how you are to pray:

Our Father in heaven,
   hallowed be your name."

From Matthew 6:5–9

❓ **Where do you pray?**

The Lord's Prayer

The name of the prayer that Jesus taught his followers is the **Lord's Prayer**. It is also called the "Our Father."

The **Lord's Prayer** is the prayer that Jesus taught his followers to pray to God the Father.

The Lord's Prayer	Meaning
Our Father who art in heaven, hallowed be thy name;	We praise God, our Father. We say God's name with love and respect.
thy kingdom come,	We pray that all people will know God's justice and peace.
thy will be done on earth as it is in heaven.	We will do what God wants, not what we want.
Give us this day our daily bread;	We ask God to give us what we need for now.
and forgive us our trespasses as we forgive those who trespass against us;	We ask God to be forgiving of us as we are of others.
and lead us not into temptation, but deliver us from evil.	We ask God to protect us from harm and keep us from sin.
Amen.	May it be so!

Activity — Share Your Faith

Think: When do you pray the Lord's Prayer?

Share: Talk about times the Lord's Prayer is prayed.

Act: Draw a place where you can pray to God. Use a separate sheet of paper.

Ways to Pray

 **Focus** **What do you say when you pray?**

Prayer is a way to deepen your friendship with God. You can pray in many ways.

- You can worship, or adore, God.

- You can praise God for all the wonders of his creation.

- You can thank God for all his gifts.

- You can tell God you are sorry when you sin.

- You can ask God for whatever help you or others need.

You can say many things when you talk to God in prayer. Sometimes you can just be quiet and enjoy being in God's love.

❓ **Which type of prayer do you say often ?**

What and When to Pray

You can use your words to pray. You can also use prayers that the Church and some of the saints have written. These prayers include the Hail Mary, the Glory to the Father, and prayers before meals.

You can pray when you are happy or sad or scared. You can pray when you are alone or with others. You can pray prayers that everyone knows, or you can make up prayers as you go.

Prayer Reminders

You can pray when you see pictures or objects that remind you that God is with you. Objects such as a crucifix, a rosary, or holy water are **sacramentals**. Words of blessing and actions, such as the Sign of the Cross, are also sacramentals.

❓ **What sacramentals do you have in your classroom? In your home?**

© Our Sunday Visitor Curriculum Division

Words of Faith

Sacramentals are blessings, objects, and actions that remind you of God and are made sacred through the prayers of the Church.

Activity — Connect Your Faith

✏️ **Write a Prayer** Write a short prayer of thanks to God. Tell what you are thankful for and why.

_____

_____

_____

_____

_____

The Lord's Prayer

 **Let Us Pray**

Gather and begin with the Sign of the Cross.

Leader: Let us pray together the prayer that Jesus taught us.

All: Our Father, who art in heaven,
hallowed be thy name;
thy kingdom come;
thy will be done on earth
  as it is in heaven.
Give us this day our daily bread;
and forgive us our trespasses
  as we forgive those who
trespass against us;
and lead us not into
  temptation,
but deliver us from evil.
Amen.

 Sing together.

O Lord, hear my prayer,
O Lord, hear my prayer:
when I call answer me.
O Lord, hear my prayer,
O Lord, hear my prayer.

"O Lord, Hear My Prayer" © 1982, Les Presses de Taizé,
GIA Publications, Inc., agent

Review and Apply

A **Work with Words** Unscramble the words and find five good reasons to pray.

1. To worship, or DRAEO God. _____

2. To ESIARP God for his greatness. _____

3. To KNATH God for all his gifts. _____

4. To KAS God for what you need. _____

5. To LLTE God you are sorry. _____

B **Check Understanding** Write your answer on the lines. What is the Lord's Prayer?

_____

_____

_____

_____

Activity   Live Your Faith

Make Up Gestures Think of a prayer that you already know. Draw stick figures to show the actions. Who is someone to whom you can teach your gesture prayer?

_____

_____

Family Faith

Catholics Believe

- Prayer is being with God in your mind and heart.

- Jesus taught his followers the Lord's Prayer.

✝ SCRIPTURE

In Luke 11:9–13 you can read another one of Jesus' teachings about prayer.

GO online www.osvcurriculum.com
For weekly scripture readings and seasonal resources

Activity

Live Your Faith

Start a Family Prayer Practice Different families have different ways of praying.

- Some pray to saints special to them.

- Others use sacramentals to pray together.

- Some have favorite customs to celebrate the seasons.

- As a group, come up with a special family prayer tradition.

People of Faith

▲ David,
ca 1000 B.C.

David was a shepherd. He was the youngest of eight sons of Jesse. God chose him to be a great leader, a king of the Israelite people. David was also a musician. He wrote psalms of adoration, praise, thanksgiving, and need. Many of these are in the Bible. People recite many of David's psalms at Mass or during their daily prayers.

Family Prayer

Dear God, help us be like David each day. Remind us to praise and adore you through our prayers. Amen.

In Unit 5 your child is learning about MORALITY.

Unit 5 Review

A Work with Words Complete each sentence with the letter of the correct word or words from the Word Bank.

WORD BANK

a. proclaim
b. work
c. faith
d. kingdom
   of God
e. Lord's

1. _____ is belief in God and all he has told us about himself.

2. The _____ is love, peace, and justice for all.

3. To _____ Jesus is to tell about him with loving words and actions.

4. The _____ Prayer is the prayer that Jesus taught us.

5. Jesus' disciples share in his life and _____.

B Check Understanding Circle the correct answer.

6. Who did Jesus call from the tree?
   Peter   John   Zacchaeus

7. Who does Jesus invite to the kingdom of God?
   everyone   saints   Catholics

8. Who is always guiding the Church's actions?
   saints   Holy Spirit   disciples

9. What name do we give to rosaries and holy water?
   sacraments   prayers   sacramentals

10. When will Jesus be with us?
    always   when we pray   when we sin

Unit 6
Sacraments

In this unit you will...

learn that the Mass is another name for the celebration of the Eucharist. The Mass has two parts: the Liturgy of the Word and the Liturgy of the Eucharist. At every Mass we hear God's word from the Bible and pray for the Church and the needs of the world. We remember Jesus' sacrifice and give thanks for it. He comes among us and renews his sacrifice. We receive his Body and Blood in Holy Communion.

Chapter 16

Chapter 17

Chapter 18

What do you think you will learn in this unit about the Eucharist?

Chapter 16 Gather to Worship

Let Us Pray

Leader: Jesus, thank you for being with us.

"For where two or three are gathered together in my name, there am I in the midst of them."

Matthew 18:20

All: Jesus, thank you for being with us. Amen.

 **Activity** Let's Begin

The Invitation Sam and his family were invited to their new neighbor Paul's birthday party. It was a big celebration. Paul's family and friends from all over the city and state gathered together. Sam was excited to meet some new people. Paul welcomed Sam and made him feel like part of the group. Together everyone had a great time.

• How do you think Paul made Sam feel like part of the group?

• When have you been to a party or event and felt welcome?

Gather to Celebrate

◎ Focus Who gathers for the Mass?

Like Paul's family and friends, the Church community gathers together. Celebrations are an important part of Church life. **Mass** is another name for the celebration of the sacrament of the Eucharist. Since the beginning of the Church, followers of Jesus have come together to worship.

✝ **SCRIPTURE**   **Acts 2:42–47**

The Community Gathers

After the Holy Spirit came, Jesus' followers met often to learn from the Apostles, to break bread together, and to pray. Some of the members sold what they had and gave the money to help the others. Still others shared their belongings with those who were in need. These followers of Jesus were very happy, and new members joined every day. Based on Acts 2:42–47

❓ **Why do you think the first followers gathered together?**

❓ **When does your parish community get together?**

The Mass Begins

Every Sunday people wave and greet each other as they walk toward their church. As they enter the church building, greeters say, "Welcome! We are so glad you are here!"

All those gathered together make up the **assembly**. Everyone gathered takes part in the Mass. They sing, pray, and use actions to worship God.

As the Mass begins, the assembly stands. They all sing a gathering song. The altar servers enter carrying a cross in a procession. The readers, deacon, and priest follow. They are singing, too.

© Our Sunday Visitor Curriculum Division

Words of Faith

Mass is another name for the celebration of the sacrament of the Eucharist.

The **assembly** is the people gathered together for worship.

Activity — Share Your Faith

Think: What are some ways you can get ready to take part in the Mass?

Share: Talk about what happens in your home or parish before Mass begins.

Act: Decide one thing you will do to welcome others at Mass next week.

Call on God

 Focus **How does Mass begin?**

After the procession ends, the priest leads everyone in making the Sign of the Cross. He greets everyone, saying, "The Lord be with you." The assembly answers in strong voices, "And with your spirit." These words and actions remind the people that Jesus is present in the priest and people gathered together.

Next the assembly recalls God's forgiveness. The priest asks everyone to think of times they may have hurt others. They ask for God's mercy. They ask God to forgive them for any wrong they have done during the week. They say together,

"Lord, have mercy.
Christ, have mercy.
Lord, have mercy."

❷ What are some ways you can show God's mercy to others?

Words of Praise

With God's forgiveness in your heart, you are better able to pray and take part in the Mass. Many times during the year, the Gloria is sung or prayed during Mass. This is a very old hymn that the Church prays to give praise and honor to God. The hymn begins with these words.

"Glory to God in the highest, and on earth peace to people of good will."

After this song, the priest invites the people to pray. The priest and assembly are silent for a few moments. The priest then prays the opening prayer, and the people respond "Amen." All gathered are now ready for the first main part of the Mass.

© Our Sunday Visitor Curriculum Division

Faith Fact

During the Easter season bells are often rung during the Gloria.

Activity Connect Your Faith

Show the Assembly Draw yourself taking part in the Mass. Label your picture.

175

Prayer of Praise

 **Let Us Pray**

Gather and begin with the Sign of the Cross.

Leader: The Lord be with you.

All: And with your spirit.

Leader: Sing joyfully to the Lord, all you lands;
serve the Lord with gladness;
come before him with joyful song.

All: We come to praise you, Lord.

Leader: Enter his gates with praise,
his courts with thanksgiving.

All: We come to praise you, Lord.

Leader: Give thanks to him; bless his name,
for he is good:
The Lord, whose kindness
endures forever.

All: We come to praise you, Lord. Amen.

Based on Psalm 100

Sing together the refrain.

We are God's
people,
the flock of
the Lord.

"Psalm 100: We Are God's
People" © 1969, 1981, and 1997,
ICEL

CHAPTER 16

Review and Apply

Check Understanding Use the numbers 1 to 5 to put the actions in the order in which they happen at Mass.

_____The altar servers, deacon, and priest process into the church.

_____The assembly begins to sing the gathering song.

_____The priest says, "The Lord be with you."

_____The assembly gathers.

_____The priest and assembly say, "Lord have mercy."

Activity Live Your Faith

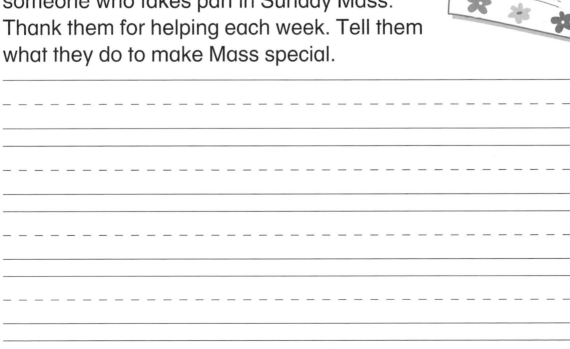

Write a Note Write a thank-you note to someone who takes part in Sunday Mass. Thank them for helping each week. Tell them what they do to make Mass special.

_____

_____

_____

_____

_____

_____

_____

_____

_____

_____

Catholics Believe

- Mass is another name for the celebration of the Eucharist.

- The assembly uses songs, prayer, and actions to worship God.

SCRIPTURE

Read Romans 12:3–8 about the different gifts people have to help serve the Lord.

GO online **www.osvcurriculum.com**
For weekly scripture readings and seasonal resources

Activity
Live Your Faith

Know the Mass Have each member of your family choose one part from the beginning of the Mass.

- Draw a picture of the part you chose.
- Display the pictures in order.
- Discuss each picture with the family.

People of Faith

Blessed Marguerite Bays spent her whole life in the neighborhood where she was born in Switzerland. She was dedicated to the sick and the poor. She called the poor "God's Favorites." At age 35, she became very ill and was miraculously cured. After that, prayer became the focus of her life. She worshipped God in everything that she did.

▲ **Blessed Marguerite Bays, 1815–1879**

Family Prayer

God, help us worship you always as Marguerite did. Amen.

In Unit 6 your child is learning about SACRAMENTS.

Chapter 17 Listen to God's Word

Let Us Pray

Leader: Lord, your word gives us hope.

"I wait for longing for the LORD,
my soul waits for his word."

Psalm 130:5

All: Lord, your word gives us hope. Amen.

Activity — Let's Begin

Story Time Andrew couldn't wait for story hour at the library. He and his friends always got there early. They wanted to sit up front so they could hear everything. Sometimes they even got to pick out the book. When the reader finished, she would ask questions about the story. Andrew loved to talk about the places and people in the stories.

• What do you like about reading or listening to stories?

The Liturgy of the Word

 Focus **What do you hear at Mass?**

Jesus learned the stories of the Jewish people. He studied Scripture and talked about God's law with wise teachers. Jesus was a wonderful teacher, too. He told many stories.

Some special stories told by Jesus are called parables. **Parables** are short stories about everyday life that help Jesus' followers learn how to love God and to follow him. Here is one parable Jesus told.

✝ **SCRIPTURE** Matthew 13:31–32

The Mustard Seed

"The kingdom of heaven is like a mustard seed that a person took and sowed in a field. It is the smallest of all the seeds, yet when full grown it is the largest of plants. It becomes a large bush, and the 'birds of the sky come and dwell in its branches.'"

Matthew 13:31–32

Jesus wanted his followers to know that the kingdom would grow with prayer and God's work.

❓ **What are some other stories Jesus teaches us?**

The Readings Begin

The first main part of the Mass is the **Liturgy of the Word**. The assembly listens to God's word from the Bible. The reader steps forward to proclaim the first reading. It is usually from the Old Testament.

Next, a singer, called a cantor, leads everyone in singing a psalm. Remember, psalms are prayers of praise found in the Old Testament.

Then, either another reader or the same reader stands and reads from one of the letters in the New Testament.

At the end of each reading, the reader says, "The word of the Lord." The assembly answers, "Thanks be to God." After each reading, everyone quietly thinks about what they have heard.

© Our Sunday Visitor Curriculum Division

Words of Faith

Parables are short stories about everyday life.

The **Liturgy of the Word** is the first main part of the Mass.

Activity — Share Your Faith

Think: What happens in your parish during the Liturgy of the Word?

Share: Talk about different ways you learn about God's word.

Act: Complete the sentence.

I learn about God's word by _____

_____

_____.

The Good News

 **Focus** What makes up the Liturgy of the Word?

Now everyone stands and sings "Alleluia!" It is time to hear the good news of Jesus Christ.

"The Lord be with you," says the priest or deacon. "And with your spirit," the assembly answers.

The priest or deacon announces what Gospel is going to be read. The Gospels contain stories about Jesus, the words of Jesus, and stories that Jesus told. The priest or deacon reads the good news of Jesus from one of the Gospels.

At the end of the Gospel, the priest or deacon says, "The Gospel of the Lord." Everyone says, "Praise to you, Lord Jesus Christ."

After the reading of the Gospel, the priest gives a homily. The homily is a short talk about the readings. It helps the people gathered understand what it means to follow Jesus.

❓ **What Gospel story have you heard recently at Mass?**

The People Speak

The assembly then stands to say the **creed** together. You say proudly that you believe in God the Father, God the Son, and God the Holy Spirit. You say that you believe in the Church and its teachings.

Next, the assembly stands together and prays the **Prayer of the Faithful**.

- You pray for the leaders of the Church and of your country.

- You pray for those who are sick and those who have died.

- You pray for people all around the world who have needs at this time.

As a leader says each prayer, you add your answer, such as "Lord, hear our prayer."

Words of Faith

A **creed** is a statement of the Church's beliefs.

The **Prayer of the Faithful** is a prayer at Mass for the needs of the Church and the world.

Activity

Connect Your Faith

Write Prayers Think of things that are happening in your family or neighborhood. Who needs your prayers right now? Fill in the blanks in these prayers.

For _____, we pray to the Lord.

For _____, we pray to the Lord.

Pray with God's Word

 **Let Us Pray**

Gather and begin with the Sign of the Cross.

Leader: Gracious God, open our hearts and minds to hear your word.

Reader 1: A reading from the First Letter of John.

Read 1 John 5:13–14.

The word of the Lord.

All: Thanks be to God.

Sing together the refrain.

Alleluia, alleluia, alleluia.

"Alleluia" © 1973, ICEL

Reader 2: A reading from the holy Gospel according to Matthew.

Read Matthew 7:7–8.

The Gospel of the Lord.

All: Praise to you, Lord Jesus Christ.

Review and Apply

Work with Words Match the description in Column 1 with the letter of the correct words in Column 2.

Column 1

1. short stories about everyday life that help Jesus' followers learn how to love God and follow him _____

2. the first main part of the Mass _____

3. what you say just before the Gospel reading _____

4. a short talk about the readings from the Mass _____

5. a statement of the Church's beliefs _____

Column 2

a. Liturgy of the Word

b. Alleluia!

c. creed

d. parables

e. homily

Activity Live Your Faith

✎ **Write a Creed** Write a prayer that tells what you believe about God.

_____

_____

_____

_____

_____

_____

_____

_____

Family Faith

Catholics Believe

- In the Liturgy of the Word, God's word is read from the Bible.

- We say what we believe about God and pray for the needs of the Church and the world.

✝ SCRIPTURE

Read Matthew 6:32 to learn about how we can count on God.

GO online **www.osvcurriculum.com**
For weekly scripture readings and seasonal resources

Activity
Live Your Faith

Read God's Word Put a Bible in a place of honor in your home. Place a candle and a crucifix nearby. Place a green plant next to the Bible to show that God's word is the living word. As a family, gather at this place this week and read a story from one of the Gospels. Then offer prayers to God for the needs of your family and friends.

People of Faith

▲ **Blessed Mariano de Jesus, 1854–1926**

Mariano was born in Colombia, South America. His parents taught him about God and his great love for the world. Even as a child Mariano taught others about God. When he became a priest, people remembered his homilies and his care for people who were poor. Pope John Paul II asked us to follow Father Mariano's example of charity, understanding, and forgiveness. Mariano was beatified in April 2000.

🙌 Family Prayer

Blessed Mariano, help us give to those who need our help. May they see God's love through our words and actions. Amen.

In Unit 6 your child is learning about SACRAMENTS.

Chapter 18 Remember Jesus' Sacrifice

Let Us Pray

Leader: God, we offer you our thanks and praise.

"I will offer a sacrifice of thanksgiving and call on the name of the LORD."

Psalm 116:17

All: God, we offer you our thanks and praise. Amen.

Activity Let's Begin

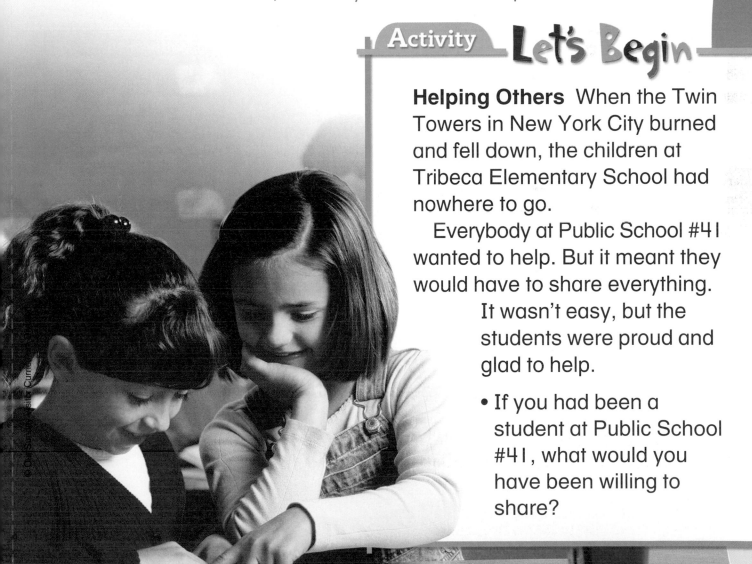

Helping Others When the Twin Towers in New York City burned and fell down, the children at Tribeca Elementary School had nowhere to go.

Everybody at Public School #41 wanted to help. But it meant they would have to share everything. It wasn't easy, but the students were proud and glad to help.

• If you had been a student at Public School #41, what would you have been willing to share?

Thinking of Others

Focus What is the sacrifice Jesus chose to make?

The children at Public School #41 made room in their hearts and in their school. They thought of others before themselves. They made a sacrifice. Sacrifice takes love and courage.

Making a sacrifice can be very difficult. A rich young man found this out when he asked Jesus about life with God forever.

✝ SCRIPTURE Matthew 19:21–22

The Rich Young Man

Jesus said to him, "If you wish to be perfect, go, sell what you have and give to [the] poor, and you will have treasure in heaven. Then come, follow me."

When the young man heard this . . . , he went away sad, for he had many possessions.

Matthew 19:21–22

The rich young man could not make the sacrifice because he loved his things more than he loved God.

❓ What is a sacrifice you have made for someone?

© Our Sunday Visitor Curriculum Division

The Greatest Gift

People make sacrifices, but Jesus chose to make the greatest sacrifice of all. Jesus' sacrifice is that he freely gave up his life on a cross to save all people from the power of sin and everlasting death. He died so that you would have new life with God forever.

God the Father rewarded Jesus for his loving choice. Through God's loving power, Jesus overcame death and was raised to new life.

The Mass is a memorial celebration of Jesus' death and Resurrection. Jesus' great sacrifice is celebrated at every Mass.

Activity

Share Your Faith

Think: What is a sacrifice you will make for Jesus?

Share: Talk in small groups about sacrifices.

Act: Write about one here.

_____

- -

_____

Give Thanks

 **Focus** What happens to the bread and wine at Mass?

The second main part of the Mass is called the **Liturgy of the Eucharist**. Those gathered remember in a special way Jesus' death and his Resurrection.

Gifts of Bread and Wine

The Liturgy of the Eucharist begins when members of the assembly bring forward the gifts of bread and wine. The people offer these gifts as a sign of their love. The priest prepares the gifts. The bread and wine will become the Body and Blood of Jesus Christ.

Now the most important part of the celebration begins. The priest leads the assembly in prayer.

Priest: "The Lord be with you."

All: "And with your spirit."

Priest: "Lift up your hearts."

All: "We lift them up to the Lord."

Priest: "Let us give thanks to the Lord our God."

All: "It is right and just."

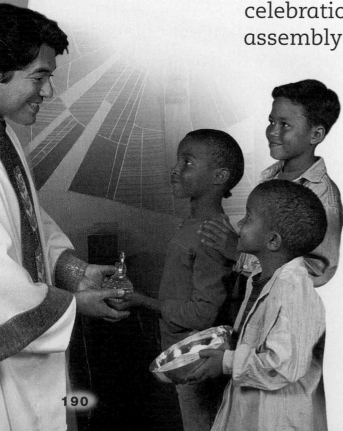

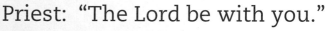

The Eucharistic Prayer

The priest now begins the **Eucharistic Prayer**. He gives thanks and praise to God. He asks the Father to send the Holy Spirit. The priest repeats what Jesus said at the Last Supper:

"THIS IS MY BODY, WHICH WILL BE GIVEN UP
   FOR YOU . . .
THIS IS THE CHALICE OF MY BLOOD, . . . WHICH WILL
   BE POURED OUT FOR YOU AND FOR MANY
   FOR THE FORGIVENESS OF SINS.
DO THIS IN MEMORY OF ME."

The bread and wine are now the Body and Blood of Christ. The assembly prays:

"We proclaim your Death, O Lord, and profess your Resurrection until you come again."

The assembly recalls all that Jesus did and offers the Father the gift of his Son. The prayer ends with everyone saying or singing the "Great Amen."

© Our Sunday Visitor · Curriculum Division

Activity — Connect Your Faith

Find the Word Find the word you say at the end of the Eucharistic Prayer. It means it is true and that you believe in what has happened. Color each X with one color and each O with a different color.

Memorial Prayer

 **Let Us Pray**

Gather and begin with the Sign of the Cross.

Leader: God our Father, your Son Jesus gave his life for us. Be with us as we pray.

Reader: A reading from the First Letter of Paul to the Corinthians.

> **Read 1 Corinthians 11:23–26.**
> The word of the Lord.

All: Thanks be to God.

Sing together.

Amen Siakudmisa.
  Amen Siakudmisa.

Amen bawo, Amen bawo,
  Amen Siakudmisa.

Amen, we praise your name,
  O God.

Amen, we praise your name,
  O God.

Amen, sing praise, Amen,
  sing praise,

Amen, we praise your name,
  O God.

"Amen Siakudmisa/Amen, We Praise Your Name"
South African traditional

Check Understanding Circle the correct answer.

1. Jesus' great sacrifice was his _____.

   birth   **death on   miracles**
                      the cross

2. The _____ become the Body and Blood of Jesus.

   cup and   words and   bread and
   plate   actions   wine

3. Jesus said, "Do this in _____ of me."

   memory   place   honor

4. At the end of the Eucharistic Prayer, the people say, _____.

   Thank-you   Amen   Alleluia

5. _____ is a memorial of Jesus' death and Resurrection.

   Baptism   Confirmation   The Mass

Activity Live Your Faith

Sacrifices People Make
Make a bulletin board or poster showing the sacrifices people make for others. Look in magazines and newspapers for pictures or stories about the people.

Family Faith

Catholics Believe

- The Eucharist is a memorial of the sacrifice of Jesus.

- The Liturgy of the Eucharist is the second main part of the Mass.

✝ SCRIPTURE

In I Corinthians 11:23–26 Saint Paul writes about the Last Supper.

GO online **www.osvcurriculum.com**
For weekly scripture readings and seasonal resources

Activity

Live Your Faith

Make Sacrifices Give each person a different color slip of paper. Have all family members write a sacrifice they will make for another family member this week. Put all the papers in a box. As each person makes a sacrifice, he or she can remove their paper from the box.

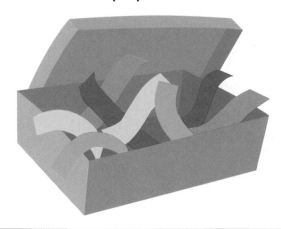

People of Faith

Giuseppe Sarto was born in Italy. He became a priest and a teacher of young men studying to be priests. In 1903 he was elected pope. He is known as the Pope of the Blessed Sacrament. He wanted young children to receive Communion daily if possible. Pope Pius X promoted Gregorian chant, which is beautiful Church music. He asked priests to give clear and simple homilies at Mass. The Church celebrates his feast day on August 21.

▲ Saint Pius X
(Giuseppe Sarto),
1835–1914

Family Prayer

Saint Pius X, pray to God for us that we may receive Holy Communion with reverence. Amen.

In Unit 6 your child is learning about KINGDOM OF GOD.

Unit 6 Review

A **Work with Words** Complete each sentence with the correct word from the Word Bank.

WORD BANK

Eucharist
Word
assembly
Mass
creed

1. _____ is another name for the celebration of the Sacrament of Eucharist.

2. In the Liturgy of the _____ stories from the Bible are read.

3. The _____ is the people gathered together for worship.

4. The Liturgy of the _____ is the second main part of the Mass.

5. A _____ is a statement of the Church's beliefs.

B **Check Understanding** Match the description in Column 1 with the letter of the correct words in Column 2.

Column 1	Column 2
6. what the assembly says at the end of the Eucharistic Prayer _____	a. Jesus' sacrifice
7. when the bread and wine become the Body and Blood of Christ _____	b. homily
8. a talk about Scripture readings _____	c. Great Amen
9. the priest or deacon reads this _____	d. Eucharistic Prayer
10. each Mass celebrates this _____	e. the Gospel

Unit 7
Kingdom of God

In this unit you will...

learn that God wants us to be one with him. The Eucharist unites us with Jesus and with one another. Because we are united, we share the same mission to love the way Jesus did. We spread the news of the kingdom of God to everyone. The Eucharist is a sign of what heaven will be like—happiness forever with God.

Chapter 19

Chapter 20

Chapter 21

What do you think you will learn in this unit about peace and happiness?

19 Share a Holy Meal

Let Us Pray

Leader: Thank you, God, for giving us what we need.
"Let the faithful rejoice in their glory,
cry out for joy at their banquet."

Psalm 149:5

All: Thank you, God, for giving us what we need. Amen.

Activity Let's Begin

Antonio's Feast Antonio lived on the eighth floor. His mother's friend Mrs. Johnson lived on the first floor. He had the measles. She made his favorite soup and climbed the stairs to take it to him.

"Everyone I passed wanted to send something along, Antonio," she said. Peeking into her basket, Antonio saw bread, olives, cheese, apples, and flowers. When he saw these things, his heart was full.

• Why did Mrs. Johnson's basket make Antonio so happy?

Prepare the Meal

 **Focus** How did Jesus share food with others?

Jesus knew how important food was for life. The Gospels have many stories of Jesus sharing meals with his friends.

SCRIPTURE
Luke 9:10-17

The Loaves and Fishes

One day Jesus was speaking to a crowd of five thousand people. Late in the day, the Apostles told Jesus to send the crowds away to nearby villages to find food.

Jesus told the Apostles to feed the people themselves. "How can we do that?" they asked. "We have only five loaves of bread and two fish."

Jesus told them to have the people sit down. He took the bread and fish, looked up to heaven, and blessed the food. He broke it into pieces and gave the pieces to his followers to pass out among the people.

Everyone had enough to eat. The leftovers filled twelve straw baskets.

Based on Luke 9:10–17

❓ **How did Jesus take care of the people?**

The Lord's Prayer

Jesus continues to feed his followers. In the Mass Jesus gives you his Body and Blood. After the assembly sings the Great Amen at Mass, it is time to prepare for a holy meal. The meal is **holy** because the bread and wine have become the Body and Blood of Christ.

The assembly stands to say or sing the Lord's Prayer. When you pray the Lord's Prayer, you pray that God will help you be more like him and you show your trust in God for all you need.

After the Lord's Prayer, those gathered offer the peace of Christ to one another. This is a sign of love and a reminder that all are united by Jesus' love.

© Our Sunday Visitor Curriculum Division

Words of Faith

Something that is **holy** is from God or shows what God is like.

Activity Share Your Faith

Think: What are some ways children your age can trust in God?

Share: Break into two groups and talk about it.

Act: Write ways you will trust in God today.

Remember Jesus

 **Focus** What happens in Mass after the Lord's Prayer?

When Jesus shared the bread and fish with the hungry people, they felt Jesus' love and care. At Mass, Jesus' followers remember Jesus' love for them as they share in his Body and Blood.

Holy Communion

After the sign of peace, the priest breaks the holy Bread before he eats it and shares it. This is what Jesus did at the Last Supper. The priest's action again reminds the assembly that Jesus died and was raised from the dead for all people.

The Body and Blood of Christ that you will receive is called **Holy Communion**. If you are free from serious sin, you are welcome at the Lord's table. When you receive Holy Communion, you are one with Jesus and all his Church.

❓ **What do you remember at Mass?**

The Body of Christ

The Body and Blood of Jesus is a great gift. When you receive it, you show **reverence**, or care and respect.

You walk to the altar prayerfully. The priest, deacon, or an extraordinary minister of the Holy Communion says, "The Body of Christ," and you say, "Amen." You receive the Body of Christ in your hand or on your tongue. You may also receive the Blood of Christ from the cup.

After you receive Holy Communion, you go back to your place and sing with everyone. Then you pray in silence.

The priest then prays the final prayer. He asks God's blessing on all gathered and sends everyone out to continue Jesus' work.

Words of Faith

Holy Communion is holy Bread and Wine that you receive in the Eucharist.

Reverence is the care and respect you show to God and holy persons and things.

Activity

Connect Your Faith

Show Reverence Draw one action at Mass that shows respect and care. Label the action.

_____

- - - - - - - - - - - -

_____

Pray with God's Word

 **Let Us Pray**

Gather and begin at the Sign of the Cross.

Leader: The Lord be with you.

All: And with your spirit.

Leader: Let us pray.

Bow your heads as the leader prays.

All: Amen.

Reader: A reading from the First Letter of Paul to the Corinthians.

Read 1 Corinthians 10:16–17.
The word of the Lord.

All: Thanks be to God.

Sing together the refrain.

I am the church! You are the church!
We are the church together!
All who follow Jesus,
  all around the world!
Yes, we're the
  church together!

"We Are the Church"
© 1972 Hope Publishing Co.

CHAPTER 19

Review and Apply

Check Understanding Use the numbers 1 to 5 to put the sentences in the order they happen at Mass.

_____ The priest breaks the bread and eats it like Jesus did at the Last Supper.

_____ All gathered pray the Lord's Prayer.

_____ The priest sends the assembly out to love and serve the Lord.

_____ The people offer one another the sign of peace.

_____ The people receive Holy Communion.

Activity Live Your Faith

Show the Body of Christ Cut out the faces of people of different ages, races, and places from old magazines. Glue them on a piece of construction paper and draw the bread and cup as a reminder that all are invited to be members of the body of Christ.

Family Faith

Catholics Believe

- Through the Eucharist, Jesus' followers are united with him and one another.

- The gift of Holy Communion is received with reverence.

SCRIPTURE

Read Romans 12:9–15 to learn how to love and serve the Lord.

GO online **www.osvcurriculum.com**
For weekly scripture readings and seasonal resources

Activity

Live Your Faith

Keep the Fast Fasting is a way to show respect and reverence for Christ in the Eucharist. The Eucharistic fast requires you not to eat or drink (except water) for an hour before you receive Holy Communion. Make a reminder poster to hang in the kitchen so that all will remember to keep the fast before Mass.

People of Faith

▲ Saint Tarsicius, third or fourth century A.D.

Tarsicius moved through Rome on a secret mission. He carried the holy Bread of the Eucharist to Christians who were in prison because of their faith in Jesus. Some people who were not Christians discovered his secret mission. They began to throw stones at him. The story of Tarsicius reminds all Catholics to respect the presence of Jesus in the Eucharist. Saint Tarsicius is the patron saint of altar servers. His feast day is August 26.

Family Prayer

Saint Tarsicius, pray for us that we may help others see the presence of Jesus in the Eucharist. Amen.

In Unit 7 your child is learning about the KINGDOM OF GOD.

Let Us Pray

Leader: Lord, we want to do your work.

"Teach me to do your will,
for you are my God.
May your kind spirit guide me."

Psalm 143:10

All: Lord, we want to do your work. Amen.

Activity **Let's Begin**

Good News Gazette

"Brother and Sister Stop Fighting"

"Girl Obeys Her Parents All Week"

"Second Graders Clean Up City Garden"

"No Stealing in Town Last Night"

"World at Peace"

"Family Helps Poor"

• What good news did you hear today?

Share the Good News

◎ Focus How can you take part in the mission of the Church?

At the end of Mass, the priest tells you to go in peace. You leave to share God's good news. Jesus' first followers took his good news to people everywhere.

✝ SCRIPTURE

Acts 10:42–48

Peter Preaches

Peter told the people of Jerusalem that Jesus sent the apostles to preach to all people.

The apostles shared the good news about God the Father, Jesus, the Son of God, and the Holy Spirit. Peter told the people that Jesus wanted everyone to believe in him. If they believed, they would receive forgiveness through Jesus' name.

After listening to Peter, many people from faraway places asked to be baptized. Peter told the crowd that anyone who was moved by the Spirit could be baptized.

Based on Acts 10:42–48

❓ **What are some things Peter might have told the people?**

The Church's Mission

Peter and the other Apostles shared Jesus' good news. Today the Church's work is to share the good news of Jesus and God's kingdom throughout the world. This work is called the Church's **mission**. All its members share in this mission.

Most Church members share Jesus' message right where they are. Others bring the message of Jesus to faraway places. They are called **missionaries**.

© Our Sunday Visitor® Curriculum Division

Words of Faith

Mission is the work of the Church.

Missionaries are people who bring the good news of Jesus and God's kingdom to people in other places.

Activity   Share Your Faith

Think: What can you do to bring Jesus' message of love to others?

Share: With a partner complete this chart.

Jesus Teaches	What You Can Do
Encourage those who are afraid.	
Help those who are weak.	
Be patient with all.	

Act: By your actions this week, share the message of love.

Called to Love and Serve

◉ Focus How did Mother Cabrini share Jesus' message?

Different people work to spread Jesus' message in different ways. Not everyone has the same gifts, but everyone can share Jesus' love.

BIOGRAPHY

A MESSAGE OF LOVE

In 1850 in a small village in Italy, Frances Xavier Cabrini was born. She was the youngest of thirteen children. Frances was sickly throughout her life, but this did not stop her from doing God's work.

Her parents read aloud the lives of the saints. Hearing the stories, Frances wanted to be a missionary in China, if God willed. Frances wanted to be a religious sister, but no group wanted her because she was sickly. So she founded her own community, the Missionary Sisters of the Sacred Heart.

❓ Why did Frances Cabrini start her own community of sisters?

Curriculum Division

Pope Leo XIII suggested that Frances go to the United States to help Italian immigrants there. Although she had a great fear of water, she crossed the ocean to New York. There she set up a home for orphaned Italian girls and other services for those who were poor.

By the time she was sixty-seven years old, Frances had set up over sixty schools, hospitals, orphanages, and convents throughout the world. In 1917 she died.

In 1946 Frances became the first United States citizen to be named a saint of the Catholic Church. She had carried out the Church's mission, bringing the love of Jesus to those in need.

Activity — Connect Your Faith

Spread the Good News You can help spread Jesus' good news. Circle two things that you will do during the next week.

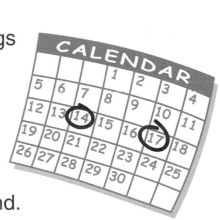

• Share your time or talent with someone who needs help.

• Pray for missionaries.

• Stand up for someone who needs a friend.

• Pray for someone who has hurt you.

• Tell someone you hurt that you are sorry.

Blessing Prayer

 **Let Us Pray**

Gather and begin with the Sign of the Cross.

Leader: Make a Sign of the Cross on your forehead. May you always remember to follow Jesus.

All: Amen.

Leader: Make a Sign of the Cross over your closed eyes. May you learn to see Jesus in all whom you meet.

All: Amen.

Leader: Make a Sign of the Cross on your lips. May all your words show respect.

All: Amen.

Leader: Make a Sign of the Cross over your heart. May love move you to action and may God give you strength to carry on the work of Jesus.

All: Amen.

Sing together.

May God bless and keep us, may God smile
   on us.
May God show us kindness, fill us with peace.
And may God bless us, Father, Son, and Spirit;
May we always love and serve, filled with
   God's peace.

Review and Apply

Work with Words Write the letter of the correct words from the Word Bank to complete each sentence.

© Our Sunday Visitor Curriculum Division

WORD BANK
a. mission
b. Frances Cabrini
c. missionary
d. Church
e. good news

1. _____ was a missionary who worked in the United States.

2. Jesus' message of God's saving love is called the _____.

3. The Church's _____ is to share the good news of Jesus and God's kingdom.

4. A _____ is a person sent to carry the good news of Jesus to people in faraway places.

5. All the members of the _____ share in its mission.

Activity — Live Your Faith

Make a Boat Try to overcome one of your fears, as Frances Cabrini did. To remind yourself of this challenge, make a boat with a bar of soap that floats, a pencil, and a sheet of paper. On the paper write your fear. (For example, fear of the dark.) Then use the paper as a sail for your boat. Let your fears float away.

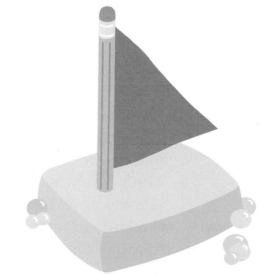

Family Faith

Catholics Believe

- The Church's mission is to share Jesus' message of love and to spread the news of the kingdom of God.

- All members of the Church share in its mission.

SCRIPTURE

Acts 1:8 tells about the Apostles' mission.

GO online **www.osvcurriculum.com**
For weekly scripture readings and seasonal resources

Activity
Live Your Faith

Serve Others' Needs As a family, look in the bulletin for the names of people who serve the needs of your parish. Also look for ways that the parish community carries on Jesus' mission by serving the needs of people in your local area. Make an action plan for taking part in your parish's service activities.

People of Faith

Anthony was born in Spain. His father taught him to weave and make designs. He also learned how to print books. Later, Anthony became a priest and then a bishop. He was a missionary in Cuba for seven years. He used all of his skills to lead people to Jesus. To be sure that his work would continue after his death, he started an order of priests, the Claretians. He also started a company that printed religious books. Saint Anthony's feast day is October 24.

▲ Saint Anthony Claret, 1801–1870

Family Prayer

Saint Anthony, pray for us that we may use our skills to teach others about Jesus. Amen.

In Unit 7 your child is learning about the KINGDOM OF GOD.

Chapter 21 Forever in Heaven

Let Us Pray

Leader: God, we want to be with you forever.
"You set a table before me...
my cup overflows." Psalm 23:5

All: God, we want to be with you forever. Amen.

Activity — Let's Begin

A Family Picnic The gathering had been nearly perfect. All the cousins were there and lots of friends, too.

The twins spent the afternoon swimming and playing. Later, everyone joined together for games. At supper the tables were loaded with all kinds of food. It was a real feast.

"Let's get the car packed up, kids," said Dad.

"Can't we stay longer?" said Jill.

"How much longer?" asked Dad.

"How about forever?" said Jesse.

• When have you wanted something to last forever?

© Our Sunday Visitor Curriculum Division

All Are Welcome

 **Focus** To what does God invite you?

Words of Faith

Heaven is life and happiness forever with God.

Jesse wanted the party to go on forever. God the Father invites everyone to the happiness of his great love in **heaven** forever. Jesus told this story to help people understand that God the Father wants everyone to enjoy this happiness.

✝ **SCRIPTURE**   Matthew 22:2–10 and Luke 14:15–23

The Wedding Feast

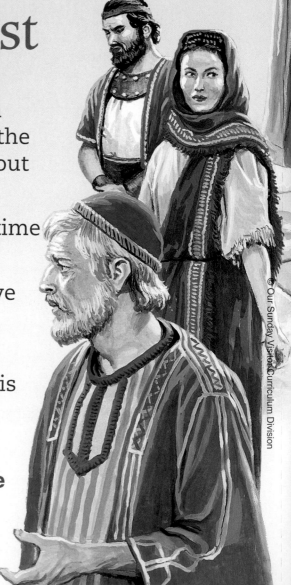

Storyteller: A king gave a wedding feast for his son. When everything was ready, the king sent his servants out to invite the guests.

Servants: The feast is ready. It's time to come and celebrate.

Three people: We can't come. We have a lot of work to do. We are very busy.

Storyteller: The servant brought this message home to the king.

❓ **What do you think the king will say? What will he do?**

King: Go out to the highways and byways. Search all the paths and alleys. Tell everyone to come. I want my house bursting with people.

Storyteller: The servants did just as the king commanded. They invited everybody to come to the banquet. And many people came. Young and old people came. People who were blind came. People who were strong helped people with crutches. Soon the house was full.

Based on Matthew 22:2–10 and Luke 14:15–23

Activity

Share Your Faith

Think: Who does the king in this story remind you of?

_____

- -

_____

Who do the invited guests remind you of?

_____

- -

_____

Share: With a partner share your answers.

Act: Break into two groups and act out the Bible story.

A Holy Feast

Focus How can you answer God's call?

God invites you to share in the great feast in heaven. In heaven you will see God face to face.

Until you see him face to face, God gives you the great gift of the Eucharist. The Eucharist is a sign of joy and of what heaven will be like. Receiving the Eucharist helps you look forward to the day when you will be with God in heaven.

Every time you receive Holy Communion, you receive the food that helps you live forever in Jesus Christ.

? **Why do you think the Eucharist is a reminder of heaven?**

Faith Fact

God made angels to be with him in heaven and to be his messengers.

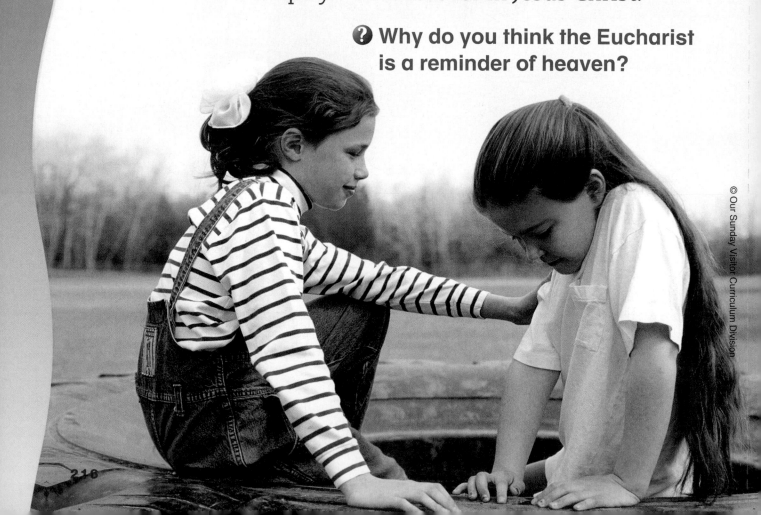

Say "Yes" to God!

God calls you to know, love, and serve him. You are like the guests in the Bible story. God invites you to share in a great feast. You can refuse to come. Or you can joyfully accept.

God invites you to say "yes" each day. Here are some ways you say "yes" to God.

- Obey the law of love.

- Listen to God's word in the Bible.

- Take part in Mass and receive Holy Communion.

- Seek God's forgiveness in the Sacrament of Reconciliation.

- Forgive and love other people.

- Help people in need.

- Pray to God each day.

Activity   Connect Your Faith

FOOD DRIVE

Answering God's Call
Living a Christian life means answering God's loving call every day. Make a list of things you do each day to say "yes" to God's invitation.

Pray with God's Word

 **Let Us Pray**

Gather and begin with the Sign of the Cross.

Leader: We rejoice that God invites us to heaven. He sent Jesus to show us the way.

Reader: A reading from the holy Gospel according to John.

Read John 3:16.

The Gospel of the Lord.

All: Praise to you, Lord Jesus Christ.

Leader: Let us pray.

Bow your heads as the leader prays.

All: Amen.

Leader: Go forth and share God's love with one another.

All: Thanks be to God.

Sing together.

Glory and gratitude and praise now let earth to heaven raise. Glory and gratitude and praise: these we offer to God.

"Glory and Gratitude and Praise" © 1994, Iona Community, GIA Publications, Inc., agent

218

Work with Words Fill in the blank with the correct word from the Word Bank.

WORD BANK

Heaven
feast
happy
Eucharist
serve

1. God wants people to be
   _____
   - - - - - - - - - - - - - - - - -
   _____ .

2. God calls us to know, love, and
   _____
   - - - - - - - - - - - - - - - -
   _____ him.

3. The _____ is a sign of
   the joy of heaven.

4. Jesus said that the kingdom of heaven is like
   _____
   - - - - - - - - - - - - - - - - -
   a great _____ .

5. _____ is life and
   happiness forever with God.

Activity Live Your Faith

Make a Door Hanger Choose one way you will say yes to God during summer vacation. Make a door hanger to remind you of what you will do. Draw a picture on it or decorate it to remind you of God's invitation to love.

Family Faith

Catholics Believe

- Heaven is life and happiness forever with God.

- The Eucharist is a sign of joy and of what heaven will be like.

✝ SCRIPTURE

Read John 17:3–5 to find out what Jesus says about life forever with God.

GO online www.osvcurriculum.com
For weekly scripture readings and seasonal resources

Activity

Live Your Faith

Spread the Message "Where charity and love are, there is God," is the line of an ancient Christian hymn. Spread some charity at home. Arrange a surprise message for one another. The message, which might be found in a lunch bag or on a pillow, might say, "Thanks for sharing your things. I like being your sister (or brother)."

People of Faith

▲ All Saints

Saints are people who put God first in their lives. They are reminders that God is calling each person to friendship and happiness with him forever. Saints chose to say "yes" to God. They chose to love and serve as Jesus did. Some saints were children. Others lived to a very old age. All the saints in heaven now see God face to face. November 1 is the feast of All Saints. On this day, Catholics remember all who are alive with God forever.

Family Prayer

All you holy saints, pray for us to God. Ask him to show us the ways of love. Amen.

In Unit 7 your child is learning about the KINGDOM OF GOD.

Unit 7 Review

A **Work with Words** Complete each sentence with the letter of the correct word or words from the Word Bank.

WORD BANK

a. heaven
b. holy
c. serve
d. mission
e. reverence

1. Something that is from God is
   _____.

2. _____ is the care and respect you show to God and holy things.

3. A _____ is the work the Church is sent to do.

4. God wants you to be with him forever in _____.

5. God calls you to know, love, and _____ him.

B **Check Understanding** Circle the correct answer.

6. A person who brings good news of Jesus to people in other places is a _____.

   missionary   priest   teacher

7. The Body of Christ received at Mass is _____.

   wine   Holy Communion   a mission

8. The first American Saint was _____.

   Frances Cabrini   Saint Peter   Pope Leo XIII

9. When you receive Holy Communion, you are _____.

   a missionary   a priest   one with the Church

10. Jesus teaches that heaven is like a great _____.
    feast   fish   Church

CATHOLIC SOURCE BOOK

The Bible

The **Bible** is God's word to people. It is one great book, made up of many small books. The word Bible means "books." Another name for the Bible is Scripture, which means "writing." The Bible has two parts.

The Old Testament

The Old Testament is the largest part of the Bible. It tells of God's love for people, especially the Jewish people, before the coming of Jesus.

The New Testament

This part tells of God's love for people after the coming of Jesus. The New Testament contains four main sections. The first section is the Gospels. The word gospel means "good news." The Gospels tell of the good news that the early Christians believed about Jesus and the kingdom of God. They are:

- The Gospel according to Matthew
- The Gospel according to Mark
- The Gospel according to Luke
- The Gospel according to John

Faith Fact

The Gospel according to Mark was the first Gospel written. It is also the shortest Gospel.

Parables

The Gospels contain stories about Jesus, the words of Jesus, words other people said about Jesus, and stories that Jesus told.

Some special stories told by Jesus are called **parables**. Parables are short stories that help people better understand a truth or mystery about God. For example, to help people better understand how much God loves all people and wants them to be happy with him forever, Jesus told the parables of the Good Shepherd, the Good Samaritan, and the King's Banquet.

Other Parts in the New Testament

- The **Acts of the Apostles** tells about the coming of the Holy Spirit and the beginning of the Christian community.

- **Letters** were written by many special people, especially Paul, who wrote to the Christian communities.

- The **Book of Revelation** was written to give hope to people who were suffering for their beliefs in Jesus.

I Believe

The **Creed** tells the faith of the Church. It brings together the Church's most important beliefs about

- God the Father, the Creator of all that is.
- Jesus, God's Son and the Savior.
- God the Holy Spirit, Giver of God's gifts.
- The Church, the Body of Christ in this world.

Nicene Creed

This creed which is prayed at Mass was written over a thousand years ago by leaders of the Church who met at a city named Nicaea. Christians over the centuries have prayed this creed.

Apostles' Creed

This creed gives a summary of the Apostles' beliefs. It is sometimes used at liturgies for children and is part of the Rosary.

The Twelve Apostles

Peter	Philip	Thaddeus
Andrew	Bartholomew	Thomas
James	Matthew	James
John	Simon	Judas

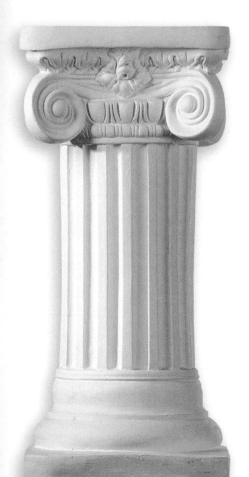

© Our Sunday Visitor Curriculum Division

The Church

The Church is the community of the People of God. Like a human body, the Church has many parts, and the parts form one body. Christ is its head, and all Christians are its members. That is why the Church is called the Body of Christ.

The Church's Mission

Before his Ascension, when he returned to his Father in heaven, Jesus told his Apostles to take his message everywhere. The Church's work is to spread the good news of Jesus and God's kingdom throughout the world.

Members of the Church

Mary is the greatest of the saints because she said yes to being the Mother of God. She has many different titles and feast days.

Other holy people are also recognized as saints. They are remembered on special days in the Church year. These are called feast days.

Everlasting Life

The Church is also a sign of the glory of heaven meant for everyone. Christians believe that there is new life with God after life on earth.

Faith Fact

Catholics are required to attend Mass on holy days of obligation. The days that are called holy days in the United States are:

Christmas, December 25

Solemnity of Mary, Mother of God, January 1

Ascension of the Lord, 40 days after Easter or the Seventh Sunday of Easter

Assumption of Mary, August 15

All Saints' Day, November 1

Solemnity of the Immaculate Conception, December 8

The Sacraments

Catholics share in the worship of the Church by participating in the Church's sacraments. The Church has seven sacraments.

Faith Fact

When you are reconciled with God and others, you have peace.

Here is the word peace in different languages.

Arabic	salam
French	paix
German	frieden
Hebrew	shalom
Italian	pace
Tagalog	katahimikan
Spanish	paz
Vietnamese	hòa bình

Sacrament	Description
Sacraments of Initiation	Baptism Confirmation Eucharist
Sacraments of Healing	Reconciliation Anointing of the Sick
Sacraments of Vocation and Service	Matrimony Holy Orders

One of the Sacraments of Healing is the **Sacrament of Reconciliation.** The Church knows that you do not always live as God wants you to live. So the Church provides the opportunity for you to experience God's love, mercy, and forgiveness in the Sacrament of Reconciliation. Through this sacrament, if you are sorry, God forgives any sins you have committed.

Celebrating Reconciliation

God's gift of conscience helps you choose right from wrong. His gift of grace, God's life within, gives you the strength to do what is right. Review the steps for this celebration.

Step 1:   Introductory rites

Step 2:   Reading from Scripture

Step 3:   Examination of conscience, litany of contrition, the Lord's Prayer

Step 4:   Individual confession, penance, absolution

Step 5:   Closing

Examination of Conscience

You prepare for the Sacrament of Reconciliation by thinking about how you keep God's Commandments and Jesus' law of love.

- Did I use God's name with respect?
- Did I show my love for God and others in some way?
- Did I usually say my daily prayers?
- Did I always obey my mother and father?

- Was I kind to those around me, or was I mean?
- Was I fair in the way that I played and worked with others?
- Did I share my things with others?
- Did I avoid taking what belongs to someone else?

- Did I care for my own things and others' things?
- Did I hurt others by calling them names or telling lies about them?
- Did I go to Mass and take part in the celebration?

Special Objects in Church

 **Altar** The altar is the table where the Eucharist is celebrated.

 **Book of Gospels** The Book of the Gospels contains the Gospel readings used at Mass.

 **Lectern (ambo)** The lectern is a stand for announcing God's word in the readings at Mass.

 **Candles** Candles lit during Mass are usually beeswax pillars. They show that Christ, the light of the world, is present.

 **Cruets** Cruets are small bottles of water or wine.

 **Chalice** The chalice is the cup for the Blood of Christ.

 **Tabernacle** The tabernacle is a container where the Blessed Sacrament is kept for those who are homebound, sick, or dying, and at Mass.

 **Ciborium** A ciborium is the special container placed in the tabernacle that holds the Eucharistic Bread, the Body of Christ.

 **Lectionary** The lectionary is a special book used at Mass that contains readings from the Old and New Testament.

 **Roman Missal** The Roman Missal is the special book that contains the prayers of the Mass.

 **Paten** The paten is the plate for the Body of Christ.

Sacrament of Eucharist

The Eucharist is a Sacrament of Initiation. It is the great thanksgiving prayer of Jesus and the Church. The Eucharist is the part of the Mass that is the Church's greatest act of worship and prayer to God. The Eucharist is also a sign of the heavenly feast that all are invited to at the end of time. The Eucharistic celebration always includes:

■ proclamation of the word of God.

■ thanksgiving to God for all his gifts.

■ the consecration of bread and wine.

■ receiving Christ's Body and Blood.

The Order of Mass

Introductory Rites
1. Entrance Chant
2. Greeting
3. Rite for the Blessing and Sprinkling of Water
4. Penitential Act
5. *Kyrie*
6. *Gloria*
7. Collect

Liturgy of the Word
The first great part of the Mass; the assembly listens to and responds to God's word in the Bible
1. First Reading (usually from the Old Testament)
2. Responsorial Psalm
3. Second Reading (from New Testament letters)
4. Gospel Acclamation (Alleluia)
5. Gospel Dialogue
6. Gospel Reading
7. Homily
8. Profession of Faith (Creed)
9. Prayer of the Faithful

Liturgy of the Eucharist
The second great part of the Mass; the Church offers thanks and praise to God
1. Preparation of the Gifts
2. Invitation to Prayer
3. Prayer over the Offerings
4. Eucharistic Prayer
   Preface Dialogue
   Preface
   Preface Acclamation
   Consecration
   Mystery of Faith
   Concluding Doxology
5. Communion Rite
   The Lord's Prayer
   Sign of Peace
   Lamb of God
   Invitation to Communion
   Communion
   Prayer After Communion

Concluding Rites
1. Greeting
2. Blessing
3. Dismissal

© Our Sunday Visitor Curriculum Division

Receiving Holy Communion

When you receive Jesus in Holy Communion, you welcome him by showing reverence. These steps can help you.

- Fold your hands and join in the singing as you wait in line.

- When it is your turn, you can receive the Body of Christ in your hand or on your tongue.

- The person who offers you Communion will say, "The Body of Christ." You say, "Amen." Step aside, and chew and swallow the host.

- You may choose to drink from the cup. When the cup is offered to you, the person will say, "The Blood of Christ." You say, "Amen." Take a small sip.

- Return to your place in church. Pray quietly in your own words, thanking Jesus for being with you.

Because it is so important to have Jesus in your life in Holy Communion, the Church tells you to receive Communion frequently. The Church especially recommends that when you go to Mass, you should also receive Jesus in Communion.

Sacramentals

As a reminder of Jesus' presence, the Church uses special signs and symbols. They are called sacramentals. A sacramental can be an object, words, or gestures.

Faith Fact

A bow, a bending at the waist of the upper part of your body, or a reverent nod of your head is a gesture of reverence and worship.

Folded hands is a traditional prayer posture. It is a sign of prayerfulness, humility, and attentiveness to the presence of God.

When you kneel, you are in a posture of adoration or sorrow. When you stand, you are showing respect.

Words
blessings
litanies
other prayers

Objects

crucifix	palms
statues	rosary
holy water	images
candles	medals

Gestures
Sign of the Cross
sign of peace
genuflection
procession

Images of Mary

Mary, the mother of Jesus, has a special place in the life of the Church. The Church honors her through special prayers, such as the Rosary, and through images, titles, and other prayers.

This stained-glass image of Mary is called "our Lady of the Blessed Sacrament."

This image of Mary comes from a church in Rome. It shows that Mary is "blessed among women" and blessed is the fruit of her womb, Jesus.

The Rosary

The rosary is a sacramental that reminds people of Mary, the mother of Jesus and that helps people reflect on the mysteries of Jesus' life and Mary's life.

The Church's Seasons

The **Church year** is a celebration of events in the life of Jesus. Every season of the Church's year has special feasts and colors and symbols.

Advent

Christians prepare to celebrate God's coming in time through Jesus, and they also recall and await Christ's coming at the end of time.

Feasts: Immaculate Conception, Our Lady of Guadalupe

Color: violet

Symbols: Advent wreath, figure of John the Baptist

Christmas

The Church remembers the birth of Jesus and celebrates the coming in time of the Son of God.

Feasts: Christmas, Epiphany, Baptism of Jesus

Color: white or gold

Symbols: manger scenes, star of Bethlehem, Jesse tree

Faith Fact

People from many countries bake Christmas cakes on the eve of the feast and eat them during the season. The cakes are thought to bring special blessings of health and good luck. Mexican *buñuelos* are an unusual pastry baked of white flour, very crisp and brittle, and eaten with honey or syrup.

Ordinary Time

The Church celebrates the words and works of Jesus. Ordinary Time occurs twice in the year.

Feasts: Corpus Christi, Transfiguration, Solemnity of Christ the King

Color: green

Symbols: vine and branches, Good Shepherd

Lent

The Church recalls our baptismal promises to change our lives through prayer, fasting, and good works.

Feasts: Ash Wednesday, Palm Sunday

Color: violet (reddish-purple); red on Palm Sunday

Symbols: ashes, stations of the cross, palms

Easter Triduum

The three most holy days of the Church, when the Church remembers Jesus' passing from death to life.

Feasts: Holy Thursday, Good Friday, Holy Saturday, Easter

Color: white or gold and red (Good Friday)

Symbols: feet washing, veneration of cross, lighting the paschal candle

Easter Season

The Church celebrates Jesus' resurrection and the new life that it brings to all.

Feasts: Ascension, Pentecost

Color: white or gold, red for Pentecost

Symbols: Alleluia, Easter lilies

God's Laws

God desires you to be in relationship with him. To help you do this and to know what is right, he has given you laws. God's laws include the Ten Commandments, the Great Commandment, Jesus' law of love, and the Beatitudes.

The Ten Commandments

THE TEN COMMANDMENTS	THEIR MEANING
1. I am the LORD your God: You shall not have strange Gods before me.	Keep God first in your life.
2. You shall not take the name of the LORD your God in vain.	Always use God's name in a reverent way.
3. Remember to keep holy the LORD's day.	Attend Mass and rest on Sunday.
4. Honor your father and your mother.	Obey your parents and guardians.
5. You shall not kill.	Care for yourself and others.
6. You shall not commit adultery.	Be respectful of every person.
7. You shall not steal.	Respect other people and their property.
8. You shall not bear false witness against your neighbor.	Respect others by always telling the truth.
9. You shall not covet your neighbor's wife.	Don't be jealous of other people's friendships.
10. You shall not covet your neighbor's goods.	Don't be jealous of what other people have.

The Great Commandment

"You shall love the Lord your God with all your heart, with all your soul, with all your strength, and with all your mind, and your neighbor as yourself."

Luke 10:27

The Beatitudes

Blessed are the poor in spirit,
  for theirs is the kingdom of heaven.
Blessed are they who mourn,
  for they will be comforted.
Blessed are the meek,
  for they will inherit the land.
Blessed are they who hunger and thirst
  for righteousness,
  for they will be satisfied.
Blessed are the merciful,
  for they will be shown mercy.
Blessed are the clean of heart,
  for they will see God.
Blessed are the peacemakers,
  for they will be called children of God.
Blessed are they who are persecuted for
  the sake of righteousness,
  for theirs is the kingdom of heaven.

Matthew 5: 3-10

Law of Love

"This is my commandment: love
one another as I have loved you."

John 15:12

Virtues

God's grace within you helps you grow in
virtue. Virtues are good spiritual habits that
strengthen you and enable you to do what is
right and good. The theological virtues are
faith, hope, and love.

Faith Fact

Symbols that
represent the
theological virtues are:

cross ⟶ faith

anchor ⟶ hope

heart ⟶ love

The Lord's Prayer

Our Father,
who art in heaven,
hallowed be thy name;
thy kingdom come,
thy will be done on earth
as it is in heaven.
Give us this day our daily bread;
and forgive us our trespasses
as we forgive those who trespass
   against us;
and lead us not into temptation,
but deliver us from evil. Amen.

Hail, Mary

Hail, Mary, full of grace.
The Lord is with you!
Blessed are you among women,
and blessed is the fruit of your womb, Jesus.
Holy Mary, Mother of God,
pray for us sinners,
now and at the hour of our death. Amen.

The Jesus Prayer

Lord Jesus Christ, Son of God,
have mercy upon me, a sinner.

Glory to the Father

Glory to the Father, and to the Son,
  and to the Holy Spirit.
As it was in the beginning, is now,
  and will be for ever. Amen.

Act of Contrition

My God, I am sorry for my sins
with all my heart.
In choosing to do wrong
and failing to do good,
I have sinned against you
whom I should love above all things.
I firmly intend, with your help,
to do penance, to sin no more,
and to avoid whatever leads me to sin.
Our Savior Jesus Christ
suffered and died for us.
In his name, my God, have mercy.

Act of Faith, Hope, and Love

My God, I believe in you, I hope in you,
I love you above all things, with all my mind
and heart and strength.

The Apostles' Creed

I believe in God,
the Father almighty,
Creator of heaven and earth,
and in Jesus Christ, his only Son, our Lord,

*At the words that follow, up to and including
the Virgin Mary, all bow.*

Faith Fact

When a pope is elected, he is given a ring with a figure of Saint Peter fishing on it. This reminds the pope that he is to be a leader of God's people as Peter was.

who was conceived by the Holy Spirit,
born of the Virgin Mary,
suffered under Pontius Pilate,
was crucified, died and was buried;
he descended into hell;
on the third day he rose again from the dead;

he ascended into heaven,
and is seated at the right hand
of God the Father almighty;
from there he will come to judge
the living and the dead.

I believe in the Holy Spirit,
the holy catholic Church,
the communion of saints,
the forgiveness of sins,
the resurrection of the body,
and life everlasting. Amen.

© Our Sunday Visitor Curriculum Division

Angel Guardian
(contemporary)

Angel sent by God to guide me,
be my light and walk beside me;
be my guardian and protect me;
on the path of life direct me.

Angel Guardian
(traditional)

Angel of God,
my Guardian dear,
to whom his love commits
    me here,
ever this day (night)
be at my side,
to light and guard,
to rule and guide.

Faith Fact

An angel is a messenger of God. Angels are mentioned nearly 300 times in the Bible. Three important angels are Gabriel, Michael, and Raphael.

Rev. Peter Klein,
The Catholic Source Book

Grace Before Meals

Bless us, O Lord, and these
    your gifts
which we are about to receive
    from your goodness, through
    Christ our Lord. Amen.

Grace After Meals

We give you thanks for all your
    gifts, almighty God,
living and reigning now and
    forever. Amen.

Morning Prayer

Blessed are you, Lord, God of all creation:
you take the sleep from my eyes
and the slumber from my eyelids.
Amen.

Evening Prayer

Protect us, Lord, as we stay awake;
watch over us as we sleep,
that awake, we may keep watch with Christ,
and asleep, rest in his peace.
Amen.

Grace Before Mealtime

Loving God, all that we have
comes from your goodness
and the work of those who love us.
Bless us and the food we share.
Watch over those who care for us.
Open our eyes to the needs of the poor.
We ask this through Christ our Lord.
Amen.

Grace After Mealtime

We give you thanks, Almighty God,
for all your gifts
which we have received,
through Christ our Lord. Amen.

Faith Fact

We also say a prayer at mealtime. We call this "saying grace." We thank God for giving us food to eat. We ask him to bless the food so we grow and stay healthy. We remember people who don't have enough to eat.

See page 241 for more mealtime prayers.

Prayer of Sorrow

Most holy and most merciful God,
strength of the weak,
rest for the weary,
comfort of the sorrowful.

[The Lord says:]
Do not fear, for I am with you.
Do not be afraid, for I am your God;
I will strengthen you, I will help you,
I will hold you in my hand. [Cf.] *Isaiah 41:10*

Prayer for the Suffering

Lord Jesus Christ, source of our life,
heal the suffering
and comfort the brokenhearted.

Faith Fact

In times of sadness it is good to pray. God will heal you and comfort you if you ask him. You can pray for someone else who is sad or suffering.

See page 239 for an example of a prayer of sorrow called an Act of Contrition.

Prayer of Community Petition

God of love, our strength and
protection, hear the prayer of
your Church.
Grant that when we come to you in
faith, our prayers may be answered,
through Christ our Lord.
Amen.

Prayer of Petition

Lord God, you know our weakness.
In your mercy grant that the example
of your saints may bring us back to
love and serve you through Christ
our Lord.
Amen.

Birthday Blessing

Loving God,
you created all the people of the world,
and you know each of us by name.
We thank you for N.,
who celebrates his/her birthday.
Bless him/her with your love and friendship
that he/she may grow in wisdom, knowledge,
  and grace.
May he/she love his/her family always
and be ever faithful to his/her friends.
Grant this through Christ our Lord.
Amen.

School Blessing

Lord God,
fill this room (school, church)
with kindness for one another
and with respect for guests.
Teach us to welcome everyone
without judgment or prejudice
but with Christian joy.
Fill us with true wisdom
which is to seek Jesus always,
now and for ever.
Amen.

Prayer for Saint Joseph's Day

Almighty God,
in your wisdom and love
you chose Joseph to be the husband of Mary,
the mother of your Son.
As we enjoy his protection on earth
may we have the help of his prayers in heaven.
We ask this through Christ our Lord.
Amen.

Prayer for Saint Valentine's Day

God our Creator,
bless the love that brings people together
and grows ever stronger in our hearts.
May all the messages that carry the name
of your holy Bishop Valentine
be sent in good joy
and received in delight.
We ask this through Christ our Lord.
Amen.

Faith Fact

When we pray with the saints, we ask them to pray to God for us and to pray with us. The saints are with Christ. They speak for us when we need help.

Prayer of Saint Francis

Lord, make me an instrument of your peace;
where there is hatred, let me sow love;
where there is injury, pardon;
where there is doubt, faith;
where there is despair, hope;
where there is darkness, light;
and where there is sadness, joy.

Litanies

Christ, hear us.
Christ, graciously hear us.
Lord Jesus, hear our prayer.
Lord Jesus, hear our prayer.

Holy Mary, Mother of God,   **pray for us**
Saint John the Baptist,   **pray for us**
Saint Joseph,   **pray for us**
Saint Peter and Saint Paul, **pray for us**

Lord, have mercy.
Lord, have mercy.
Christ have mercy.
Christ have mercy.
Lord have mercy.
Lord have mercy.

Faith Fact

A litany is a prayer with one line that is meant to be repeated over and over again so that those praying are caught up in the prayer itself.

© Our Sunday Visitor Curriculum Division

Sign of the Cross

In English
In the name of the Father,
and of the Son,
and of the Holy Spirit.
Amen.

In Latin
In nomine Patris,
et Filii,
et Spiritus Sancti.
Amen.

Glory to the Father

In English
Glory to the Father,
and to the Son,
and to the Holy Spirit:
as it was in the beginning,
is now,
and will be forever. Amen.

In Latin
Gloria Patri,
et Filio,
et Spiritui Sancto.
Sicut erat in principio,
et nunc, et semper,
et in saecula saeculorum. Amen.

Faith in Action!
CATHOLIC SOCIAL TEACHING

Faith in Action!
CATHOLIC SOCIAL TEACHING

Care for Creation

God calls you to protect his gifts and to use them wisely. You show God respect when you take care of the planet and all that is in it.

God wants people to have the water, the food, and the air they need to live. The things people do today can help save God's gifts for people to use many years from now.

❓ What are some ways you can care for God's creation?

Helping water the plants

Recycling!

Taking care of Stanley

Adopt a Lake

Everything needs water to live and grow. Let's look at what one community did to care for God's special gift of water.

Children in a school in Lakeland, Florida, found their own way to care for creation. The Catholic school children worked with their community to clean up a lake. Their program was called Adopt a Lake.

Families spent a Saturday cleaning up a lake. They picked up trash. They removed harmful plants. They put signs up to remind people to care for the lake. These children showed how important it is to care for God's special gift of water.

❓ How did the children take care of God's creation?

Reach Out!

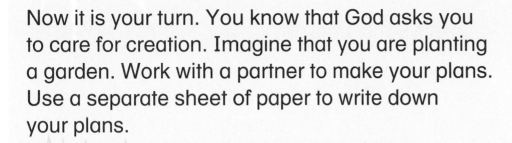

Plan a Garden

Now it is your turn. You know that God asks you to care for creation. Imagine that you are planting a garden. Work with a partner to make your plans. Use a separate sheet of paper to write down your plans.

1. List three things you would like to grow.

2. List things you need for the garden.

3. What does the garden need to keep growing?

4. How would you share your garden?

Make a Difference

Clean a Playground Work together as a class to clean up the school playground. Then talk to first-grade classes about why you cleaned the playground. Invite other classes to find a way to care for God's creation at your school.

DISCOVER

Catholic Social
Teaching:

Life and Dignity
of the Human
Person

Faith in Action!
CATHOLIC SOCIAL TEACHING

Respect Each Person

God created you in his own image. There is no one else exactly like you. God blessed you with many gifts and talents. God did this for everyone!

Sometimes it is easy to forget this good news. You think of the things you can't do, or the things you don't like about someone else. God calls you to treat all people, yourself included, with respect. You are wonderfully made!

❓ **How can you show respect for yourself?**

❓ **How can you show respect for others?**

Wonderfully Made

Every person deserves respect. Let's look at how some special children are learning that they are wonderfully made.

Jason cannot do math. Megan cannot walk or talk. Danny can't sit up.

These children, and others like them who have special needs, live at St. Joseph's Center in Pennsylvania. The people who work at St. Joseph's can give these children the care they need. The staff of St. Joseph's Center helps the children see themselves with God's eyes. They remind the children that they are wonderfully made. The workers at St. Joseph's and the children's families see with God's eyes. They do not worry about what the children can't do. They see only what the children can do.

Jason can give the best hugs. Megan smiles at everyone. Danny tells everyone he loves them.

> ❓ **How do you think the children at St. Joseph's Center feel about themselves?**

Reach Out!

Write a Letter

Now it is your turn to help someone see that he or she is wonderfully made. Think of someone you know who needs to hear this good news. Use a separate sheet of paper to write this person a letter. In your letter, follow these steps.

1. Tell the person why you care for him or her.

2. Name some of the gifts and talents that make the person special.

3. Tell the person that he or she is wonderfully made in God's image.

Make a Difference

Collect Toys or Blankets Work together as a class to collect new stuffed toys or blankets, or used ones in good condition. Share the toys or blankets with children in a local hospital or homeless shelter. Talk to a first-grade class about your project. Invite other classes to find ways to show respect for all people.

DISCOVER

Catholic Social
Teaching:

Rights and
Responsibilities of
the Human Person

Faith in Action!
CATHOLIC SOCIAL TEACHING

Rights and Responsibilities

Humans need many things to live happy and healthy lives. Some of these things are:

- a safe place to live.
- healthful food and clean water.
- health care.

These important things are called **human rights**. All people deserve to have these needs met.

The Church teaches that humans have rights because they are made in God's image. Each person has the responsibility to make sure other people get what they need. We are called to protect the human rights of all people.

❓ **What are some ways that people can make sure others get what they need?**

© Our Sunday Visitor Curriculum Di

Peter Takes Responsibility

Sometimes people's rights are not protected. Let's look at how one holy man took responsibility for helping others.

Peter Claver was born in Spain, hundreds of years ago. He became a priest. Peter felt called by God to travel halfway around the world to South America. He wanted to share God's love with the people of Colombia.

When Peter got off the ship in the port of Cartagena, he saw a terrible sight. Men, women, and children from Africa had been taken from their homes to be sold as slaves. They were hungry, sick, and frightened.

Peter spent the next forty years caring for these people. He helped them get food and clothing. He cared for them when they were sick. Peter could not end slavery, but he took responsibility for doing what he could to help. He became known as "the slave of the slaves." Today we call him Saint Peter Claver.

❓ How did Saint Peter Claver show that he believed all people have rights?

258

Reach Out!

Make a List

Saint Peter Claver did his best to help those who were harmed by slavery. At your age, you cannot do much to change the world. Right now, you can do things to make people happier and healthier, close to where you live.

On a separate sheet of paper, make a list of ways you can be responsible at home and at school. Think of things that will help others Here are some ideas to get you started.

- Watch out for younger children on the playground.

- Make sure your pet has food and clean water every day.

Make a Difference

Make New Friends With your teacher's help, learn more about children in another school, town, state, or country. Exchange class letters or e-mail. Tell the other children about your neighborhood and your school. Ask the other children to tell you about their lives.

Dear New Friend,

Faith in Action!
CATHOLIC SOCIAL TEACHING

Respect for Workers

Work is an important part of human life. People work to earn money for the things they need. Workers take pride in doing their jobs well.

Jesus learned about work from his foster father, Joseph. Joseph was a carpenter who made beautiful and useful things from wood. Jesus also watched his mother, Mary, as she worked hard to make a loving home for the family.

The Church teaches that all kinds of work are important. Workers and bosses have to treat one another with respect. Everyone who works deserves to be paid fairly. No one should work in unsafe conditions.

❓ **Who are some of the workers who help make your life safe, comfortable, and interesting?**

We Wear Their Work

All workers should be treated with respect. Let's look at what some U.S. college students did to help.

Do you have a favorite tee-shirt? Most young people do! But have you ever thought about where that shirt was made?

Many clothes are made here in the United States. Other clothes sold here are made in other countries around the world. Often these factory workers work long hours for little pay. They are not treated with respect.

Many groups in this country are trying to do something about these bad working conditions. One group trying to help is the Worker Rights Consortium (con-SORE-tee-um). They ask American colleges and universities to buy items only from companies who treat their workers well.

The next time you wear your favorite tee-shirt, think about the person who made that shirt. Ask God to make his or her working conditions better.

❓ **How does the Worker Rights Consortium help workers in clothing factories?**

Reach Out!

Lemonade
5¢
Help Workers

Do Your Part

You may think you are too young to help change the lives of workers. Because of you, workers may get better working conditions and the respect of the people for whom they work. Here are some ideas you and your family might try.

Skip-a-Snack Save the money you might use to buy snacks at school or at a movie for one month. Ask your family to help you send the money to the Worker Rights Consortium or Catholic Charities to be used to help workers.

Yard Sale Organize a yard sale with your family. Invite friends' families to join, too. Sell lemonade and cookies. Make cards or other crafts to sell. Tell your customers you are raising money for the rights of workers around the world.

Make a Difference

Write a Class Letter Workers in this country often need help, too. With your teacher's help, write a class letter to the president or to your state senators. Ask elected leaders to help pass stronger laws that protect the health and safety of workers of all ages.

Dear
Mr. President

Faith in Action!
CATHOLIC SOCIAL TEACHING

One Human Family

The members of the human family, like the members of your family, may not all look alike. People have different skin colors. They speak different languages. They live in very different places. All humans are part of one family.

Just as you care for your brothers and sisters at home, Jesus sends us to care for our brothers and sisters around the world. That's one big job! One way to begin is to remember that everyone is made in God's image. Another way to care for our sisters and brothers around the world is to pray for them.

❓ **What are some other ways you can show that you care for all the members of the human family?**

Twins!

Being a twin is a special blessing. Twins have a special way of being close. They grow up together and help one another.

Did you know that whole parishes can be twins? Holy Spirit Catholic Church in Virginia has a twin parish in the country of Haiti. The people of Holy Spirit Parish and the people of Our Lady of Mount Carmel Parish near Port-au-Prince, Haiti, chose to have a special, close relationship. The two parish communities help each other like twins.

Caring for the human family starts right where we live. Let's look at how the people of one parish reached out to their sisters and brothers in another country.

Haiti is a poor country. The people of Holy Spirit Parish send gifts of food, medicine, and machinery to their twin parish. In return, the people of Our Lady of Mount Carmel Parish share their faith and their joy. Visitors who travel from one parish to the other are welcomed like family—because they are!

❓ **What do you think the members of these twin parishes teach each other?**

Reach Out!

Learn about the Human Family

One way to show that you care for all members of the human family is to learn about people in other parts of the world. Choose a country you want to learn about. Use library books or the Internet to find out about this country. Answer these questions on a separate sheet of paper.

1. What are three ways in which the people are like you?

2. What are three ways in which the people are different from you?

3. What could you learn from the people?

4. What could you teach them?

Make a Difference

Have a Cultural Festival Make a list of all the cultures and countries represented in your class. Hold a festival of cultures. Wear clothing from the country you learned about. Share special foods, music, and customs. Invite another class to celebrate with you.

DISCOVER

Catholic Social
Teaching:

Call to Family,
Community,
and Participation

Faith in Action!
CATHOLIC SOCIAL TEACHING

Get Involved!

God made people to live in families and communities. People need other people to share God's love. You are part of your own family, and part of the family of all God's people. You are part of many communities— your neighborhood, your school, your parish, and the Church around the world.

It is good to know that you are not alone. The gifts of family and community come with responsibilities, too. God calls everyone to take part in family and community. We need to help others so no one is left out, and no one feels alone.

❓ What is one way you are involved in your family and one way you are involved in a community?

Making Room

Do you remember the Christmas story? Jesus was born in a shelter for animals, because there was no room at the inn.

Everyone is called to get involved in family life and community life. Let's see how the members of one parish community are reaching out to those who feel alone.

Every year in wintertime, homeless people must feel the way Mary and Joseph did—alone, cold, and left out. There are often many more homeless people living on the streets than there are places for them to stay. In Tennessee, a Catholic priest saw homeless people sleeping outside in the cold. He thought about Mary and Joseph. So he started a program called Room in the Inn. In the winter, churches welcome homeless people to sleep on church property, and they give them meals.

❷ **How does the Room in the Inn program help homeless people?**

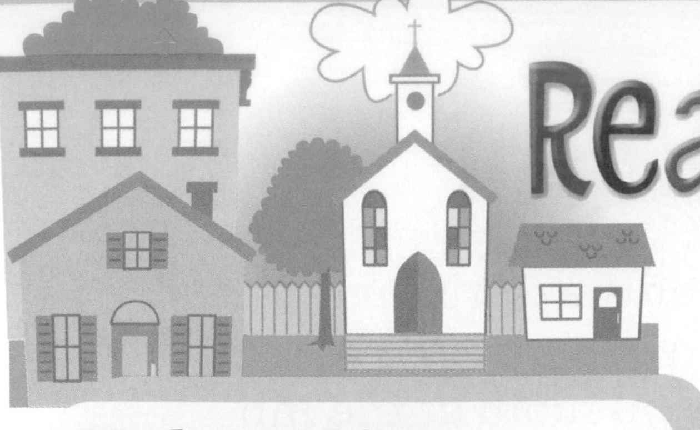

Make a List

Name three ways you take part in the life of your family and your community. With a partner, name three ways your class could take part.

Ways I Take Part

1. _____

2. _____

3. _____

Ways the Class Takes Part

1. _____

2. _____

3. _____

Make a Difference

Help Your Community   Find out what helpful events your community has planned. Work as a class to help—by raising money for walkers or runners, baking cookies for a bake sale, helping to wash cars, or making signs. Invite other classes to join you.

Faith in Action!
CATHOLIC SOCIAL TEACHING

Those Most in Need

One day Jesus was talking with his disciples. They asked him how they could follow him more closely. Jesus told them, "Whatever you do for your brothers and sisters who are most in need, you do for me. When you care for them, you care for me. When you turn your back on them, you turn your back on me." (Based on Matthew 25:31–46)

Jesus asks us to use the same message. "Look for those who need your care the most," Jesus says. "When you reach out to help them, you will find me."

❷ **Who are the people in your community who are most in need?**

© Our Sunday Visitor Curriculum Division

Bags Full of Love

Katy knows what it is like to be a foster child. A foster child can't live with his or her family for a while for some serious reason. Foster children are taken in by other caring families. Sometimes they return to their families. Other times they may be adopted into new families. Katy was a foster child. She was blessed to have a loving family adopt her.

When Katy was preparing for Confirmation, she knew exactly what she would do for her Christian service project. Katy knew that many foster children don't have suitcases or backpacks to carry their things when they leave home. Sometimes they have to carry things in grocery sacks or plastic trash bags. So Katy decided to help.

Katy bought colorful tote bags. She filled the bags with stuffed animals, school supplies, and other things foster children need. She made sure every foster child in her community had a bag of his or her own—a bag filled with love.

❷ How did Katy reach out to others?

Reach Out!

Make a Collage

Now it is your turn to look for the face of Jesus in those who are in need. Copy or cut out a picture of Jesus. Glue the picture to a poster board. Then look through old magazines for pictures of people who are in need, or people who are helping others. Cut out the pictures and glue them around the face of Jesus.

Hang your finished poster at home to remind you to look for Jesus in others.

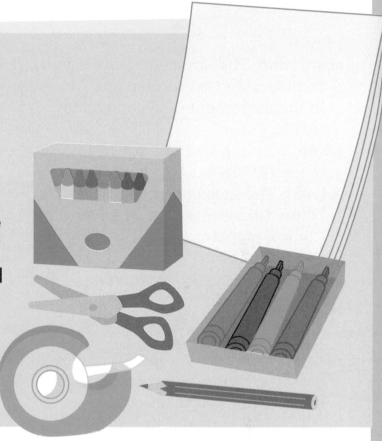

Make a Difference

Pack Your Bags Work together as a class to pack lunches for children in a local daycare center or family shelter. Or fill plastic food storage bags with personal items, such as washcloths, toothbrushes, toothpaste, and soap, or school supplies. Send the bags to a place that help children in need.

WORDS OF FAITH

A

absolution The forgiveness of sin you receive from God through the Church in the Sacrament of Reconciliation. (131)

adore Worship God. Adoration is a form of prayer. (164)

Advent The season of four weeks before Christmas. During Advent the Church prepares to celebrate the birth of Jesus. (136)

assembly The people gathered together for worship. (173)

B

Baptism The sacrament that makes the person a child of God and a member of the Church. It takes away original sin and all personal sin. (121)

Bible The word of God written in human words. There are two parts to the Bible, the Old Testament and the New Testament. (59)

C

Church The community of all baptized people who believe in God and follow Jesus. The word is often used for the Catholic Church. (87)

Church year The celebration in the liturgy of events in the life of Jesus. (136)

conscience A gift from God that helps you know right from wrong. (104–105)

consecration Through the power of the Holy Spirit and the words and actions of the priest, the gifts of bread and wine become the Body and Blood of Jesus. (191)

contrition Being sorry for sin and wanting to live better. (129)

creation Everything made by God. (42–43)

creed A statement of the Church's beliefs. (183)

D

disciples People who choose to follow Jesus. (86–87)

E

Easter The Church's celebration of the Resurrection of Jesus from the dead. The celebrations at the Easter Vigil on Holy Saturday and on Easter Sunday mark the Church's greatest holy day, Easter. (139)

Eucharist The sacrament in which Jesus shares himself and the bread and wine become his Body and Blood. (172)

Eucharistic Prayer The great prayer of thanksgiving prayed by the priest in your name and that of the Church. (191)

faith Belief in God and all that he has told about himself. (147)

God the Father A name for God that tells God's great love for people. God the Father is the first Person of the Holy Trinity. (71)

God the Holy Spirit The third Person in the Holy Trinity. The Holy Spirit is a guide who helps people stay close to God. (87)

grace A sharing in God's life. (121)

Great Commandment Jesus' law to love God above all else and to love others the way you love yourself. It sums up all God's laws. (95)

heaven Life and happiness forever with God. (214)

holy From God or something that shows what God is like. (199)

Holy Communion Holy Bread and Wine that you receive in Eucharist. (201)

Holy Family The name for Jesus, Mary, and Joseph. (78–79)

Holy Trinity A name for the three Persons in one God—Father, Son, and Holy Spirit. (85)

homily A short talk about the readings at Mass. (182)

kingdom of God Love, peace, and justice for all. (148–149)

Last Supper The meal Jesus shared with his followers on the night before he died. (191)

Lent The season of forty days during which the Church gets ready for Easter. It is a time of prayer, good actions, and sorrow for sin. Lent begins with Ash Wednesday. (138)

liturgy The public worship of the Church. It includes the Sacraments and forms of daily prayer. (136–137)

Liturgy of the Eucharist The second main part of the Mass. (191)

Liturgy of the Word The first main part of the Mass. (181)

Lord's Prayer The prayer that Jesus taught his followers to pray to God the Father. (163)

Mass Another name for the celebration of the Sacrament of the Eucharist. (172–173)

mercy Loving kindness and forgiveness. (112–113)

mission The work of the Church. (207)

missionaries People who bring the good news of Jesus and God's kingdom to people in other places. (207)

Mortal Sins Serious sins that cut people off from God's life. (105)

New Testament The second part of the Bible that tells of the life and teaching of Jesus, his followers, and the early Church. (61)

Old Testament The first part of the Bible that is about God and his people before Jesus was born. (59)

original sin The first sin committed by the first people. (51)

parable Short stories about everyday life. (180–181)

penance A prayer or an act to make up for sin. (131)

Pentecost The day the Holy Spirit first came upon the disciples and the Church. (139)

praise Giving God honor and thanks because he is good. Praise is a form of prayer. (42)

prayer Talking to and listening to God. (71)

Prayer of the Faithful Prayer at Mass for the needs of the Church and the world. (183)

proclaim To tell about Jesus with loving words and actions. (155)

psalm A prayer from the Bible; it can be said or sung. (42)

reverence The care and respect you show to God and holy persons and things. (201)

Resurrection The mystery of Jesus being raised from death. (139)

sacrament A holy sign that comes from Jesus and gives life. (121)

sacramentals Blessings, objects, and actions that remind you of God and are made sacred through the prayers of the Church. (165)

Sacraments of Initiation The first sacraments that are celebrated by new members of the Church: Baptism, Confirmation, and Eucharist. (123)

Sacrament of Reconciliation The sacrament in which God's forgiveness for sin is given through the Church. (130–131)

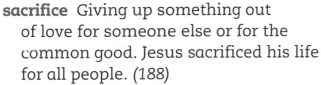

sacrifice Giving up something out of love for someone else or for the common good. Jesus sacrificed his life for all people. *(188)*

saint A holy person who obeyed God and followed Jesus. *(69)*

Savior The one sent into the world to save people who were lost through sin and to lead people back to God. *(52–53)*

sin Choosing to disobey God. It is doing what you know is wrong. *(44–45)*

Son of God The name of Jesus that tells you God is his Father. *(45)*

Temple The holy building in Jerusalem where the Jewish people came to worship God. *(78–79)*

Ten Commandments God's laws about loving God and others. *(94–95)*

The Three Days The most holy time of the Church year—Holy Thursday, Good Friday, Holy Saturday, and Easter Sunday. It celebrates Jesus' passing through death to life. *(28)*

trust To believe in and depend on someone. *(71)*

venial sins Less serious sins that do not completely remove a person from God's life and love. *(105)*

Illustration Credits

Paul Bachem 42-43, 79; Dan Brown 78, 84-85, 172-173, 155; David Cabot 62-63; Olivia Cole 45, 87, 139, 191; Carolyn Croll 20-21; Bob Dombrowski 58-59; Allen Eitzen 32-33; Barbara Kiwak 44-45, 76-77, 148-149; Dennis Lyall 36-37; Geoff McCormack 208-209; Diane Paterson 12-13, 105, 208; Karen Patkau 50-51, 180-181; Roger Payne 8-9, 102-103, 214-215; Francesca Pelizzoli 86; Larry Schwinger 70-71, 110-111, 146-147; Joel Spector 52-53; Clive Spong 128-129, 198-199, 206-207; Arvis Stewart 24-25, 96-97, 188-189; Matt Straub 43, 48, 56, 69, 73, 89, 95, 99, 103, 113, 115, 116, 123, 125, 126, 133, 137, 141, 149, 152, 159, 167, 173, 177, 183, 186, 189, 193, 194, 199, 203, 209, 211, 215, 217, 219; Walter Stuart 94, 154-155; Susan Swan 122; Meryl Treatner 120-121; Douglas Van Fleet 20-21; Lois Woolley 48, 56, 64, 74, 82, 90, 100, 108, 116, 126, 134, 142, 152, 160, 168, 178, 186, 194, 204, 212, 220, 178.

Photo Credits

iv Ariel Skelley/Blend Images/Corbis; 1 l Jo Foord/DK Images; 1 r Rubberball Productions/Getty Images; 2 Jon Feingersch/Masterfile; 6-7 bg Myrleen Ferguson Cate/Photo Edit; 7 inset Father Gene Plaisted, OSC; 10-11 bg LF File/Shutterstock Images LLC; 11 t Photodisc/Getty Images; 11 b Tom & Dee Ann McCarthy/Corbis; 14-15 bg Sally Brown/Index Stock Imagery/Photolibrary; 15 bg Corel; 15 fg Richard Hutchings; 16-17 bg Hans Georg Roth/Corbis; 16-17 fg SW Productions/Getty Images; 18-19 Richard Hutchings/Corbis; 22-23 fg Richard Hutchings; 23 bg Mitchell Funk/Getty Images; 26-27 bg Corel; 27 bl Photos.com; 27 br Stephen Simpson/Getty Images; 28-29 Stephanie Maze/Corbis; 30-31 bg Stephanie Maze/Corbis; 31 fg Richard Hutchings; 34-35 Bryan F. Peterson/Corbis; 35 inset Stockbyte/Getty Images; 38-39 Roger Tidman/Corbis; 40 l Adamsmith/Getty Images; 40 c Lisette Le Bon/SuperStock; 40 r Jon Feingersch/Masterfile; 40-41 bg Adamsmith/Getty Images; 45 Steve Satushek; 46 Raoul Minsart; 47 Rommel/Materfile; 49 Lisette Le Bon/SuperStock; 54 Neil Beer/Photodisc/Getty Images; 55 l Stockbyte/Getty Images; 55 c Digital Vision/Getty Images; 55 r Pedro Coll/Age Fotostock; 57 Jon Feingersch/Masterfile; 59 Creatas/Age Fotostock; 61 Our Sunday Visitor Curriculum Division; 62 Myrdal Mase/Getty Images; 66 l AJA Productions/Getty Images; 66 c Daniel Pangbourne/Getty Images; 66 r Zave Smith/Age Fotostock; 66-67 bg AJA Productions/Getty Images; 69 Photo Courtesy of Salesian Missions; 72 Jose Luis Pelaez, Inc./Corbis; 75 Daniel Pangbourne/Getty Images; 77 David Young-Wolff/PhotoEdit; 80 Richard Hutchings; 82 Catherine Yeulet/iStock; 83 Zave Smith/Age Fotostock; 85 t Myrleen Ferguson Cate/PhotoEdit; 85 b Father Gene Plaisted, OSC; 87 Michael Keller/Corbis; 88 Bill Wittman; 90 SW Productions/Punchstock; 92 l Charlie Edwards/Photodisc/Getty Images; 92 c Graham French/Masterfile; 92 r Kevin Dodge/Masterfile; 92-93 bg Charlie Edwards/Photodisc/Getty Images; 95 Philip Gould/Corbis; 97 Richard Hutchings; 98 Banana Stock, Ltd./Punchstock; 101 Graham French/Masterfile; 104 Raoul Minsart/Masterfile; 106 Bill Wittman; 108 Nancy Sheehan/Index Stock Imagery/Photolibrary; 109 Kevin Dodge/Masterfile; 112 Richard Hutchings; 113 Richard Hutchings; 114 Father Gene Plaisted, OSC; 118 l Stockbyte/Getty Images; 118 c Photodisc/Getty Images; 118r Justin Pumfrey/Carrie Beecroft/Getty Images; 118-119 bg Stockbyte/Getty Images; 121t Father Gene Plaisted, OSC; 121 b Ryan McVay/Getty Images; 123 Father Gene Plaisted, OSC; 124 Father Gene Plaisted, OSC; 127 Photodisc/Getty Images; 129t Bill Wittman; 129 b

Andreas Kuehn/Getty Images; 130 l Father Gene Plaisted, OSC; 130 r Bill Wittman; 131 Myrleen Ferguson Cate/PhotoEdit; 132 Michael Keller/Corbis; 134 ULTRA.F/Digital Vision/Getty Images; 135 Justin Pumfrey/Carrie Beecroft/Getty Images; 136 Richard Hutchings; 137 t Peter Holmes/Age Fotostock; 137 b Burke/Triolo/Brand X Pictures/Punchstock; 138 Richard Hutchings; 139 Father Gene Plaisted, OSC; 140 Rubberball Productions; 142 Jeff Greenberg/Index Stock Imagery/Photolibrary; 144 l Richard Hutchings; 144 c Dan Lim/Masterfile; 144 r Richard Hutchings; 144-145 bg Richard Hutchings; 149 Myrleen Ferguson Cate/PhotoEdit; 150 Kevin Dodge/Masterfile; 151 Roy Ooms/Masterfile; 153 Dan Lim/Masterfile; 156 t Alvaro Leiva/Age Fotostock; 156 c Paul Barton/Corbis; 156 b Arthur Tilley/Getty Images; 157 l Father Gene Plaisted, OSC; 157 r Bill Wittman; 158 David Noton; 160 Gabrielle Revere/Getty Images; 161 Richard Hutchings; 162 Bill Wittman; 164 t Frank Siteman/Getty Images; 164 b Thinkstock/Getty Images; 165 Jim Corwin/Index Stock Imagery/Photolibrary; 166 Michael Newman/PhotoEdit; 168 Myrleen Ferguson Cate/PhotoEdit; 170 l Ronnie Kaufman/CORBIS; 170 c David Pollack/CORBIS; 170 r David Schmidt/Masterfile; 170-171 bg Ronnie Kaufman/CORBIS; 173 Bill Wittman; 174 Father Gene Plaisted, OSC; 175 Richard Hutchings; 176 Kevin Dodge/Masterfile; 178 Stuart Pearce/AgeFotostock; 179 David Pollack/CORBIS; 181 t Bill Wittman; 181 b Myrleen Ferguson Cate/PhotoEdit; 182 Father Gene Plaisted, OSC; 183 Bill Wittman; 184 Digital Vision/Getty Images; 187 David Schmidt/Masterfile; 189 Bill Wittman; 190 Myrleen Ferguson Cate/PhotoEdit; 191 Father Gene Plaisted, OSC; 192 A & F Pears, Ltd., London/SuperStock; 196 l Jose Luis Pelaez, Inc./CORBIS; 196 c Massis J. Boujikian/Corbis; 196 r Roger Tully/Getty Images; 196-197 bg Jose Luis Pelaez, Inc./CORBIS; 199 Father Gene Plaisted, OSC; 200 Spencer Grant/PhotoEdit; 201 Myrleen Ferguson Cate/PhotoEdit; 202 Bill Wittman; 204 Burke/Triolo Productions/Getty Images; 205 fg Massis J. Boujikian/Corbis; 205 bg The Copyright Group/SuperStock; 207 Victor Maqque; Courtesy Maryknoll Mission Archives; 209 bg Courtesy of Missionary Sisters of the Sacred Heart of Jesus Stella Maris Province, New York City; 209 fg C Squared Studios/Photodisc/Getty Images; 210 Bill Wittman; 212 David Young-Wolff/PhotoEdit; 213 Roger Tully/Getty Images; 216 Bill Wittman; 217 tl SW Productions/Getty Images; 217 br Myrleen Ferguson Cate/PhotoEdit; 218 Digital Vision/Getty Images; 220 Rick Gomez/Masterfile; 222-223 Richard Hutchings; 224 KAI PFAFFENBACH/Reuters/Corbis; 226 NASA-GSFC; 228 tl Digital Imaging Group; 228 tr Digital Imaging Group; 228 tcl Digital Imaging Group; 228 tcr Digital Imaging Group; 228 bcl Digital Imaging Group; 228 bcr Digital Imaging Group; 228 bl Digital Imaging Group; 228 br Digital Imaging Group; 229 tl Digital Imaging Group; 229 tr Digital Imaging Group; 229 b Digital Imaging Group; 231 Bill Wittman; 232 t Photos.com; 232 c Photodisc/Getty Images; 232 b Richard Hutchings; 233 t Father Gene Plaisted, OSC; 233 b Arte & Immagini srl/Corbis; 234 l Father Gene Plaisted, OSC; 234 r Photos.com; 235 l Corel; 235 r Corel; 237 PhotoSpin; 238-239 Thinkstock/Getty Images; 240-241 Thinkstock/Getty Images; 242-243 Thinkstock/Getty Images; 244-245 Thinkstock/Getty Images; 246-247 Thinkstock/Getty Images; 248-249 Thinkstock/Getty Images; 250 l Juice Images/Corbis; 250 l James Shaffer/PhotoEdit ; 250 l Adrian Arbib/Corbis; 250 l Randy Taylor/Index Stock/Photolibrary; 250 l Peter Turnley/

Corbis; 250 l Royalty-Free/Corbis; 250 l Myrleen Ferguson Cate/PhotoEdit; 251 t Louise Tanguay; 251 bl Tom Stewart/Corbis; 251 bc Myrleen Ferguson Cate/PhotoEdit; 251 br Michael Newman/PhotoEdit; 251 bg Stuart Westmorland/Corbis; 252 t fivespots/Shutterstock Images LLC; 252 bl Juice Images/Corbis; 253 fg David Laronde/Corbis; 253 bg Stuart Westmorland/Corbis; 254 t Bill Aron/PhotoEdit; 254 b Kevin Radford/Masterfile; 254 bg Frank Krahmer/Getty Images; 255 James Shaffer/PhotoEdit ; 257 t Adrian Arbib/Corbis; 257 b Bill Aron/PhotoEdit; 259 Reed Kaestner/Corbis; 260 t Jose Luis Pelaez, Inc./Corbis; 260 b Richard Hutchings/PhotoEdit; 260 bg VisionsofAmerica/Joe Sohm/Getty Images; 261 Randy Taylor/Index Stock/Photolibrary; 263 Digital Vision/Getty Images; 264 c Alyx Kellington/Index Stock/Photolibrary; 264 bl Michele Burgess/Index Stock/Photolibrary; 264 br Peter Turnley/Corbis; 266 t Mark Richards/PhotoEdit; 266 b Hutchings Stock Photography/CORBIS; 267 Royalty-Free/Corbis; 269 Myrleen Ferguson Cate/PhotoEdit; 270 Courtesy Jackie and Katy Carpas

Acknowledgments

For permission to reprint copyrighted material, grateful acknowledgment is made to the following sources:

International Consultation on English Texts: English translation of Glory to the Father (the *Gloria Patri*), Lord, have mercy, the Apostles' Creed, the Lord's Prayer, Lamb of God (*Agnus Dei*), and *Kyrie eleison* by the International Consultation on English Texts (ICET).

Liturgy Training Publications, 1800 North Hermitage Avenue, Chicago, IL 60622, 1-800-933-1800, www.ltp.org: From "Meal Prayer for Harvest Time" (Retitled: "Grace Before Mealtime"), "Prayers for Sad Days" (Retitled: "Prayer of Sorrow"), "Prayer for Times of Crisis" (Retitled: "Prayer for the Suffering") and "Epiphany Blessing of a Gathering Space" (Retitled: "School Blessings") in *Blessings and Prayers through the Year: A Resource for School and Parish* by Elizabeth McMahon Jeep. Text © 2004 by Archdiocese of Chicago: Liturgy Training Publications.

Twenty-Third Publications, A Division of Bayard: "Grace After Meals" (Retitled: "Grace After Mealtime") from *500 Prayers for Catholic Schools & Parish Youth Groups* by Filomena Tassi and Peter Tassi. Text copyright © 2004 by Filomena Tassi and Peter Tassi.

United States Conference of Catholic Bishops, Inc., Washington, D.C.: "At Bedside" (Retitled: "Evening Prayer") and "Washing and Dressing" (Retitled: "Morning Prayer") in *Catholic Household Blessings and Prayers.* Translation copyright © 1989 by United States Catholic Conference, Inc. From the English translation of "Blessing on Birthdays or the Anniversary of Baptism" (Retitled: "Birthday Blessing") in *Book of Blessings.* Translation copyright © 1988 by United States Catholic Conference, Inc.